THE
HERBAL
GROVE

THE
HERBAL
GROVE

Mary Forsell

**PHOTOGRAPHS BY
TONY CENICOLA**

VILLARD
NEW YORK • 1995

This book contains descriptions of historic usages of herbs and is not intended as a medical reference. For treatment, herbal or otherwise, for medical problems, please seek the advice of a physician or herbalist. Also bear in mind that some people may experience an allergic reaction to plant materials and essential oils called for in recipes, so it is advisable to proceed carefully and with good common sense when preparing and using them.

Library of Congress Cataloging-in-Publication Data

Forsell, Mary.
The herbal grove / by Mary Forsell ; photographs by Tony Cenicola.
p.   cm.
Includes bibliographical references and index.
ISBN 0-679-40841-X (alk. paper)
1. Tree crops.   2. Trees—Utilization.   3. Plants, Useful.   4. Herbals.
5. Cookery.   I. Title.
SB170.F67 1994
582. 16'063—dc20   93-46156

Manufactured in Italy on acid-free paper

9 8 7 6 5 4 3 2

First Edition

DESIGNED BY BARBARA MARKS

FOR ALBERT

ACKNOWLEDGMENTS

Many thanks to Emily Bestler, my editor, and Molly Friedrich, my agent, for their spirited support and guidance. Thank you, too, Amelia Sheldon, for keeping things on course, and Linda Greer, for her detailed recipe testing.

And then there were all those people, spread across thousands of miles, who shared their knowledge and offered their help. They are:

Tom Bates, curator, Museum of Beverage Containers and Advertising, Goodlettsville, Tennessee

Mary Chiltoskey and Goingback, Cherokee, North Carolina

Commercial Office of Spain, New York City

Dianne David of Stolen Flowers, Austin, Texas

Señora Vida de Aguirre, El Cigarral de Cadena, Toledo

Fred Hicks, president of Hicks Nurseries, Inc., Westbury, Long Island, New York; Joel Albizo and Jack Siebenthaler, American Association of Nurserymen, who contributed so many useful tips for how to plant and care for trees

Alexander and Elena Deutsch, Los Angeles, California

The staff of *Foxfire*

Lucas Guardiola, Tur Madrid

Hotel Villa Real, Madrid

Jas. Kirkland, Williamsburg, Virginia

The Loom Company, New York City

Nuñez del Prado, Baena, Spain

Yvonne Owens, Victoria, British Columbia

Jeff Poppen, Long Hungry Creek Nursery, Red Boiling Springs, Tennessee

Rare Pit and Plant Council and Debbie Peterson, New York City

Camille Stagg, Chicago

Adam and Sue Turtle of Earth Advocates, Livingston, Tennessee

Jean Pierre Vandelle, chef and owner, El Olivo, Madrid

Pilar Vico and Ada Newman, Tourist Office of Spain, New York City

A fond thank you to those who contributed their favorite herbal tree recipes:

Clara Maria Amezúa de Llamas, Alambique Cooking School, Madrid (Spanish Citrus Toast, Xato Sauce, and Almond Cookies, pp. 57, 118, and 119)

Hector and Susie Black of Hidden Springs Nursery, Cookeville, Tennessee (Real Elderberry Jelly, p. 140)

Naomi Black, New York City (Sweet Potato–stuffed Maple Pork, Apple Gingerbread, pp. 35 and 84)

Casa Botin, Madrid (Pacharan, p. 11)

Ryan Drum, Waldron Island, Washington (Honied Rowan Berries, p. 146)

Rafael Fornell, chef, and Juan Muñoz Estévez, Colombia Tipico Restaurante, Granada, Spain (Almond-Garlic Soup, p. 117)

Dora Gerber, Swissette Herb Farm, Salisbury Mills, New York (Swiss Mountain Tea, p. 106)

Cyrus and Louise Hyde, Well-Sweep Herb Farm, Port Murray, New Jersey (Spicy Greek-style Stew, p. 76)

Joel Jason of the catering firm In Your Kitchen, New York City (Walnut–Wheat Berry Salad and Orange Chicken Breasts with Pomegranate, pp. 73 and 133)

Eduardo Martin, director, Paradis, Madrid and New York City (Marinated Shrimp Carpaccio, p. 95)

Steven Mazarky, Green Shutters Restaurant, Clayton, Georgia, who researched classic Southern uses for sourwood honey, which we photographed at his restaurant (p. 97)

Carol McGrath, Victoria, British Columbia (Balm of Gilead Salve, p. 111)

Vicente F. Orts Llopis, and Santiago Orts Perez, Jardineria Huerto del Cura, Elche, Spain (Date-Almond Tapas, p. 101)

Barbara Reimensnyder Duncan, Ph.D., Hearts o' Flowers, Franklin, North Carolina, for her tour of Southern flora as well as her recipes (Carolina Allspice Perfume Cream, Black Walnut Cake, and Peach Butter, pp. 44, 74, and 125)

Restaurante Sevilla, Granada, Spain (where we photographed Sorbetto al Limone, p. 56)

Lynne Tolley and Mary Ruth Hall, Miss Mary Bobo's Boarding House, Lynchburg, Tennessee (Lemon Icebox Pie and Lynchburg Peach Pie, pp. 55 and 126)

Mo Tomodante, Applewood Farmhouse Restaurant, Sevierville, Tennessee (Juice Julep and Apple Fritters, pp. 82 and 83)

Abousabah Waja, El Caballo Rojo, Cordoba, Spain (where we photographed Ajo Blanco and Almond Tart, pp. 116 and 120)

Jannelle Wilkins, Altamira Tours, Denver, Colorado (Citrus Salad, p. 58)

Contents

Introduction

Most people have memories of favorite childhood trees. Who has not had a "pet" tree to observe, climb, or just sit beneath? There is certainly an emotional link between people and trees, which arguably stems from our ancestral beginnings in their boughs. Trees are intimately associated with the history of civilization. Stone Age man feasted on elderberry flowers and berries. The olive tree has been a strong economic force in the Mediterranean for more than four thousand years, due to its rich harvest of fruits and oil. When the Grecian olive trade surpassed that of Phoenicia, that land was doomed to obscurity. Incense-yielding frankincense and myrrh trees were extremely profitable for the ancient land of Punt, now Somalia, where they still grow abundantly. Seventeenth-century Arabians got rich on the coffee trade, and without the coffee tree, Brazil could not have prospered so enormously in the nineteenth and twentieth centuries.

Trees are also local landmarks and commemorate the life and times of small towns with such common names as the Lover's Oak or the Hangman Cottonwood. There are also notable trees of historical significance, such as the Sam Houston Kissing Bur Oak in San Marcos, Texas, under which Houston gave campaign kisses when he was running for senator; the Buckman Tavern Norway Maple in Lexington, Massachusetts, where the Minutemen discussed strategies; the Falcon Hurst Silver Maple in Franklin, Tennessee, under which Southerners hid their valuables from the Union army; the John Ruskin Live Oak of Ocean Springs, Mississippi, where the English poet meditated on an American visit; and the Treaty Live Oak of Jacksonville, Florida, where many agreements were struck between white settlers and Native Americans.

Trees have been venerated since antiquity. Sacred groves were planted in their honor in places as diverse as Persia and Finland. Royalty has been coronated beneath their boughs. These stately, remarkable plants have always embodied and symbolized permanence. Dark, lush glades have an air of mystery; orchards in bloom are rustically romantic; and gardens graced with antique shade trees are timeless in their beauty. The tree is unequaled among plants for both its size and longevity, which can stretch to centuries. Trees shelter and shade and also provide a canopy to sit under or a limb to swing from. Their beauty, the texture of their trunks, their whispers in the wind, and the heady scents of their needles, leaves, and flowers seduce the senses.

The flaming colors of the maple in autumn, the lacy charm of the first dogwood blossoms of spring—these are unforgettable sights and among the strongest images that come to mind when we think of trees. But the tree has more to contribute than its beauty. Since the beginning of civilization, the tree has been a principal player in the herbal repertoire. Herbs are traditionally thought of as low-growing, leafy plants and flowers that can be harvested and used for their flavors, scents, and medicinal benefits. However, trees offer the same wonderful gifts as the smaller herbs—leaves, flowers, and roots, as well as the delightful bonuses of bark and fruit.

This book, inspired quite spontaneously one day by a drive through an indescribably fragrant eucalyptus-lined road in northern California, is about the many uses of trees. A major portion of it is dedicated to recipes, from soups to desserts, that are enhanced by the different seasonings which trees and shrubs provide. There are also recipes for wonderful household applications made from ingredients found in trees. For example, the strange-looking fruits of the Osage orange can be used to prevent insects from taking up residence in your home, and balm of Gilead buds are a perfect all-natural air freshener. If you are tired of depending on store-bought perfumes or packaged skin-care treatments, you might want to try the cosmetic recipes included, such as Carolina Allspice Perfume Cream and the Almandine Facial Mask.

A white willow gracefully provides shade in a horse pasture. Though willows prefer a moist soil, they'll flourish wherever the ground isn't too dry and where there's lots of sun. People as diverse as the ancient Greeks and Native Americans have used willow as a painkiller. Today, herbalists prescribe decoction of willow bark for fever.

Throughout this book, there are also discussions on the medicinal usages of leaves, bark, and fruit. These are simply outlined for you. Seek the help of an herbalist to carry the treatment further. Beyond these traditional remedies, there are also emerging medicinal applications made from different parts of common trees. Scientists recently began testing the yew (*Taxus canadensis*) for cancer-fighting qualities, tea tree oil is appearing in skin preparations more and more, and cosmetic companies are emphasizing natural ingredients, such as elder flower, in their products. Even people who do not have the resources to grow the trees discussed in this book can buy the herbal products derived from them from an herbalist or even a grocery store. The gifts of the tree are every-where—use them in good health.

Just as they've thrived for centuries in the Mediterranean, citrus flourish today in a square in the middle of Valencia, Spain—one of the first regions in the world to make citrus fruits a commercial venture. Oranges were once considered a novel luxury fruit and were broken out like champagne or special chocolates for the holidays.

THE
HERBAL
GROVE

THE LINEAGE AND LORE OF THE HERBAL TREE

A grove of birches in
northern Europe
brings to mind the
days of Druid
worship in forests.
One of the
harbingers of spring
because of its early
show of leaves, the
birch was the first
tree in the ancient
Celtic tree alphabet,
symbolic of the
beginning of the
lunar year, just after
the winter solstice.

THE LINEAGE AND
LORE OF
THE HERBAL TREE
3

It's impossible to discuss history without acknowledging the role trees have played in it. From antiquity, the tree has been associated with wisdom. In the East, the Buddha is said to have gained enlightenment under the pipal, a kind of fig tree, while in the West, Isaac Newton had his own gravitational insights under the apple, and, for better or worse, went on to create calculus and other mathematical disciplines. Creation myths of India, such as those in the Upanishads, are told by forest-dwelling sages. The Druids, who were the priestly, intellectual class of Celts two thousand years ago, held their festivities and ceremonial gatherings in woodland clearings. Similarly, centuries ago in Germany, people commonly gathered in groves for ceremonial worship of nature spirits.

Significant trees mentioned in the Bible include the olive, juniper, willow, pomegranate, and myrtle. The Israelites actually had laws protecting trees—a practice they shared with the Hittites of the second millennium B.C., who severely punished tree abusers. Furthermore, in some areas of west Africa, the simple act of pruning a cola tree is considered irreverent to the tree spirit. It is believed that when the tree flowers, the imprudent pruner or planter will surely die. In Scandinavia, the same miserable fate awaits anyone who chops down an elder tree.

In many cases, beliefs about the fortune-telling abilities of trees arose from their peculiar responses to the weather. One case in point is the rain tree of India, which moves its leaves sideways in rain or darkness. In the Appalachian region of North America, the fruits of the serviceberry signal the approach of spring and the "services" that traditionally come with the season, such as visits of clergy or doctors to the house.

Beliefs in Europe regarding trees and tree spirits are centuries old. The rowan tree—whose berries have a high vitamin C content—is associated with the

Finnish god of thunder. Norsemen once built their homes around growing trees such as the rowan for protection against both evil spirits and the forces of nature. Ancient people residing in what is now Marseilles, France, actually made human sacrifices to trees.

Wherever they grow, trees beautify the landscape and influence the cuisine of entire cultural communities that surround them.

CHINA

In China, herbalism has been practiced for more than five millennia and is thought to have first been recorded under the auspices of the Emperor Shen Nong. The *Pen-ts'ao Kang-mu*, the first Chinese herbal, is attributed to Shen Nong and is reputed to date from the third millennium B.C., although recent studies have shaved about one thousand years off that estimate. Shen Nong, with a life so steeped in legend it is hard to separate the mythic events from the real ones, is believed to have shunned the daily pleasures of court life to dabble in herbal remedies. However, his writings show that he did much more than dabble. He recorded almost four hundred herbal substances, many of which later found a place in Western herbalism.

There is another surviving Eastern medicinal text, written around 1000 B.C., known as the *Wu Shi Er Bing Fang,* or "Prescriptions for Fifty-two Diseases." So vital was this book that it was often buried with the dead, presumably to ensure good health in a postterrestrial realm. In tomb excavations this herbal has been found alongside corpses clutching magnolia blossoms, *Magnolia lili flora* (for the unopened buds' decongestant properties), the inner bark of the cinnamon tree, *Cinnamonum cassia* (for its toxin-releasing abilities), and seeds of the *Ziziphus* tree, sometimes known to Westerners as Chinese jujube or Chinese date (for their sedative effect on the liver).

As the centuries passed, Chinese medicine became linked with the basic Taoist spiritual philosophy of opposing yet complementary forces at work in every aspect of life. Beginning around 500 B.C., this interdependent, yin-yang credo was applied to medicine, diet, and exercise. Physical health was elevated to a spiritual plane for Taoist monastics who followed strict diets and martial-arts regimes. As a result, spirituality became interwoven with Chinese herbal medicine. Doctors treated ailments by balancing patients' inner energy. Also, as Chinese spiritual philosophy became linked increasingly with medicine, further interrelationships were traced between the body and the universe itself. For example, the heart became associated with fire and the apricot, the liver with wood and the plum, the lungs with metal and the pear.

By the Tang Dynasty in the seventh century, Chinese herbalism had developed into a sophisticated science. The legendary Dr. Sun Simiao, who practiced during this time, was so renowned for the success of his treatments that he was invited by a succession of emperors to serve as their personal physician. He declined and instead worked his herbal magic on the citizens at large, mostly practicing preventive medicine by encouraging good dietary habits.

Although Marco Polo certainly did much in the thirteenth century to make the Western world aware of Chinese herbalism, it wasn't until the publication of the *Ben Cao Gang Mu,* the life work of Li Shi-Zhen, in the sixteenth century— and its subsequent translation into a variety of European languages in the seventeenth century—that this body of knowledge was widely disseminated.

Contemporary Chinese herbalism is governed by the same yin-yang principles and treats yin illnesses (inner-body ailments and diseases of the chest and lower organs) with yang solutions (those governing the back, upper body, and everything outside the body) and vice versa. Thus, the bark of the Chinese cinnamon tree (*Cinnamonum cassia*), which aids such yin organs as the liver and spleen, is employed for yang deficiency. The clove tree (*Syzygium aromaticum*), which has a yin affinity with the lungs and stomach, is also useful for yang deficiency. In contrast, the Chinese jujube (*Ziziphus jujuba*), associated with the skin—a yang domain—is medicinal for the yin. Some plants are not necessarily yin or yang: the immature fruits of the immensely attractive but thorny Chinese orange (*Poncirus trifoliata,* not a true orange) are used to keep energy (*qi*) balanced.

Many of the treatments are administered through herbal teas, honey pills, and broths. Yet, as with the medicine practiced by Dr. Sun Simiao in the seventh century, most contemporary Chinese medicine is preventive and depends primarily on simple balances of foods at meals. Westerners can observe this concept at work at its most basic level in a Chinese meal consisting of hot or spicy foods followed by cooling oranges for dessert.

Numerous trees are used in Chinese herbalism, many of which you will find in the pages that follow. There is a growing movement by Western herbalists to recognize the healing value of fruits that the Chinese herbalists have been utilizing for these purposes for millennia. The fruits of quince, hawthorn, ginkgo, dogwood, and mandarin orange, for example, are all important elements of the Chinese herbal repertoire.

Egypt

In ancient times, frankincense was a valuable commodity and was carefully stored in sealed jars, brought out only for embalming, fumigation, and temple rites.

The twenty-eighth dynasty of ancient Egypt (circa 1570–1342 B.C.) was a time of momentous cultural development, exploration, and territorial expansion. It was during this period that Egyptian gardens reached their pinnacle of opulence, were arranged in geometric patterns, and contained trees bearing such luxurious edibles as dates, pomegranates, and figs. The Egyptians also developed specialized temple gardens, many of them containing plots devoted exclusively to herbs. Frankincense and myrrh were important plantings in the herb plot, for the incense derived from them was essential to ceremonial activities.

It was during this time in Egyptian history that Queen Hatshepsut came to power. Anxious to impress the Egyptian world with her prowess as a ruler, she exercised no moderation as she made her palace—and, in particular, her personal temple garden—the most spectacular in the land. The queen sent an expedition to Punt—now known as Somalia—to gather luxury items. Along with such animate treasures as monkeys and giraffes, the expedition crew also sought coveted goods such as frankincense and myrrh. It is recorded in the reliefs on her temple walls that these incense trees were transported with the greatest of care, with their root balls intact. Planted in the temple garden, the trees helped to strengthen the reputation of the palace as a healing place, inspiring many disease-stricken citizens to make pilgrimages to the site.

When the average ancient Egyptian citizen needed medical attention, there were several options available. If the problem was straightforward, such as a wound or a broken leg, an ordinary physician would treat the patient in much the same way we know today—with bandages, ointments, and splints. Some diseases were thought to be cured with specific botanicals, such as figs for the heart, Egyptian plums (*Cordia myxa*) for the lungs, juniper berries for indigestion, and burned willow leaves mixed with oils for skin ailments.

If the illness was too mysterious to diagnose, the afflicted would visit a magician, who would attempt to cure it with incantations and potions. No matter what the problem, it was likely that a tree would be used in some way in the curing process. While the physician might mix *Ziziphus* tree leaves with honey as a wound bandage, the magician was likely to begin his spell-casting by burning olive wood to create a proper mystical atmosphere. After he got a good smoke going, the magician would mix up a potion. A common one combined frankincense, myrrh, cinnabar, mulberry juice, rain water, and wormwood juice. The magician would then anoint the ailing person's body with this concoction while reciting a spell.

If none of this worked, the last option was to visit a temple, such as Queen Hatshepsut's, to seek relief. Predating both the monastery and the rejuvenating spa, these temples offered overnight accommodations in lovely rooms scented with slow-burning myrrh (which also repelled insects) and a chance for the afflicted to commune with healing spirits while slumbering and emerge refreshed. Of course, a stroll around the frankincense-and-myrrh–scented garden during daylight hours also expedited recovery.

In Egypt, the tree could also be counted on for general protection. Cautious citizens placed branches of acacia in their homes to protect them from thieves. Meanwhile, in southwest Asia, Arabs were seeking similar protection by summoning the god Al-Ozza with sacred offerings of acacia branches.

Life-giving as they were, herbal trees were also essential in elaborate Egyptian rituals surrounding death. Attendees of the upper-crust Egyptian funeral banquets would often wear floral collars made from a papyrus backing filled with olive leaves, date palm leaves, cornflowers, woody nightshade berries, red cloth, and beadwork. Herbal trees were also a key resource for preparing mummies.

The most expensive embalming process was a meticulous procedure involving myrrh, cassia, and a number of spices. A less expensive one called for oil of cedar.

Ancient Greece and Rome

Herbs—and the herbal tree, in particular—flourished in ancient Greece and Rome. Both cultures were highly instrumental in developing the folklore that surrounds these plants today, and also for discovering their medicinal, culinary, and household usages.

The Greeks rewarded their athletes with crowns fashioned from the laurel (bay) tree. They honored Aphrodite with myrtle, and also used the plant medicinally, adding it to therapeutic drinks, with perhaps a bit of pomegranate, another culturally important tree. They surrounded their homes with lovely tree-filled groves. Because water was never abundant, Greek gardeners favored evergreens, such as laurel, myrtle, pine, and rosemary. Fig and olive trees flourished in the stony Greek soil and were an integral part of their gardens. They also valued all kinds of fruit trees, which were as symbolic of gods as they were useful in the kitchen. A description of a garden belonging to a regal citizen appears in Homer's *Odyssey*, written sometime between the eighth and ninth centuries B.C. The tony garden, filled with trees conducive to a comfortable Grecian lifestyle, is called Alcinous and is described in Book VII as follows:

> Outside the courtyard, near the entrance, is a great garden of four acres with a fence bordering it on each side. Here tall, thriving trees are planted—pears, pomegranates, apples with glistening fruit, sweet figs, rich olives. The fruit of these trees never fails in any season of the year. . . .

As did other ancient peoples, the Greeks cultivated sacred groves of both a highly manicured and a wild nature to honor their vast collection of gods.

A recognizable pattern persists in the lineage of the sacred grove. This style—orderly rows of trees punctuated by pools and flowers—was originally cultivated by the Egyptians, who later inspired the Persians, who, in turn, influenced the Greeks. Such fruitful groves influenced Roman garden design

The ancient Greeks were passionately fond of evergreen groves, and physicians such as Dioscorides experimented freely with potentially healing herbal concoctions harvested from their boughs.

and helped spawn the *villa rustica,* or agricultural estate, which was watched over by the garden goddesses Minerva and Venus. On such estates, shimmering groves abounded, sometimes equipped with rustic tree seats nestled within the boughs for an afternoon of arboreal contemplation.

Trees also contributed to the Roman medicine chest. Dioscorides, who worked as an army doctor, mentioned many herbal remedies in his *De materia medica* of circa A.D. 65. He wrote of a tonic comestible that involved roasting a viper with spicery and fruits of the fig tree.

Herbal trees were also essential ingredients in Roman cuisine, which relied upon a rich balance of seasonings. Cinnamon bark was especially prized but was absurdly expensive because it had to be imported through a costly spice-trading route. Nevertheless, Romans happily imported cinnamon for cookery and for certain burial rituals.

EUROPE

For herbs in general, the medieval period was anything but a dark age. Rather, it was a time when an incredible number of new plants were imported into Europe, courtesy of European contact with the Middle East during the Crusades. Monks launched into feverish experimentation as they worked to keep up with the herbal immigration.

The monks of St. Gall—a monastery dating from the year 820—laid out their gardens with the Roman villa style in mind. They grew a variety of fruit and nut trees in the orchard adjacent to the cemetery. The herb garden was nearby, as was the infirmary, where the monks doctored the sick with preparations derived from both the medicinal plot and the orchard.

The typical medieval monastic garden was likely to contain medicinal and culinary herbs, vegetables, dye plants, and fruit trees, in particular pear and quince, which is an herbal tree known for its ethereal pink springtime petals. Tapestries of the medieval period often depict serene garden scenes with such trees as linden, holly, aspen, and English oak; around each scene might run a border of pomegranates.

During the medieval period, beliefs in northern Europe and England regarding the healing properties of trees abounded. In hopes of a cure, people actually made Chaucerian-style pilgrimages to famous trees—usually ones with peculiar clefts or odd features, such as holes formed by the meeting of two branches. Such magical trees were named for their physical characteristics—*arbre à trou* (hole tree) or *arbre fourcher* (forked tree) in France, and *Zweiselbaum* (tree with two parts) in Germany.

The golden age of herbals coincided with the reign of Queen Elizabeth I (1558 to 1603). Preceded by the works of such German herbalists as Otto Brunfels and Leonhard Fuchs in the 1530s, it is the British herbals—a bit more chatty and slightly more outrageous than their German counterparts—that continue to fascinate us today. One of the most famous is Nicholas Culpeper's work, *The Complete Herball.* Culpeper, who dabbled in astrology long before it entered the realm of tabloid literature, developed and popularized a method of relating plants to planets. For Culpeper, the birch was ruled by Venus, the willow tree by the Moon, and the elm by Saturn. He then devised treatments based on the relationship between each planet and specific body parts. For example, he recommended boiling the bark of the black alder with other herbs to cure dropsy, applying elm root as a treatment for baldness, and placing willow boughs in a sickroom for the cooling effect they have on a bedchamber.

Although the influence of herbals diminished from the seventeenth century onward—as the apothecary's magic was replaced by more scientific methods—beliefs about certain plants' healing properties continued to thrive.

As late as the eighteenth and nineteenth centuries in England, many people continued to believe in the magic of trees. Sick people continued the medieval practice of being "passed through" the V opening of a split tree, usually a maple, in order to be cured or to attract good luck. People also still visited a shrew ash in Surrey, which was also called the Sheen Tree, to seek cures for their sick children.

Close cousin to cherries and plums, blackthorn (Prunus spinosa) yields the sloe berry, used to flavor sloe gin. Over the last thirty years, another blackthorn-related beverage, made in Spain and called pacharan, has been gaining repute throughout Europe as a stomach-fortifying tonic. Made from soaking vitamin-C-rich blackthorn fruits (sloes) in anisette for at least three but no more than five months, the rosy pink beverage recalls the ancient European monastic tradition of brewing medicinal liqueurs.

In NEW WORLDS

In the nineteenth century, British citizens began to relocate to the oldest and smallest continent, Australia. They wrote home of the odd plant and animal life there, including the peculiar platypus, the curious kangaroo, and, of course, the mint- and lemon-scented groves of giant eucalyptus trees, which were also called peppermint gums, bloodbark, and ironbark. Savored by the koala—another Australian oddity—the eucalyptus is used by Aborigines, who smoke the leaves to treat asthma. British settlers added eucalyptus oil to boiling water and breathed in the steam to treat colds. (Such practices still exist: Fresh branches of eucalyptus placed in a steam room freshen the air and unblock nasal passages, and eucalyptus is an essential oil in aromatherapy.)

Across the sea on the strange, unexplored North American continent, the Europeans found plenty of new herbal trees. Many of the Europeans' new-found cures were based on Native American healing practices. Native tribes had their own favorite herbal trees. They used, among others, eastern hemlock as a liniment for rheumatism, a decoction of eastern red cedar fruit to treat coughs, and an infusion of speckled alder bark to treat eye irritations.

The native tribes taught the pioneers how to brew roots for healing teas, use witch hazel to treat skin ailments, cook with sassafras, substitute white pine and other tree bark for ordinary food in times of famine, use the inner bark of slippery elm to soothe a sore throat and even butternut sap as a sweetener.

The settlers selectively borrowed Native American recipes, both culinary and medicinal, and integrated them into their Old World household routines. They freshened their linens with leaves of the sweet fern shrub, used the very ripe fruit of persimmon to plump up and sweeten their cakes and brew beer, savored sweet honey locust pulp and made tea from the pods (a practice not recommended today because of the tree's toxicity), made blue dyes from the bark of red maple, and used New Jersey tea leaves as a tea substitute (useful in times of heavy taxation).

The woods provided the ingredients for many beverages: spring beer called for sassafras, spicewood, and other woodland-growing plants; spruce beer was made with both black and white spruce; fruits of the hop tree (*Ptelea trifoliata*) were used as a substitute for hops vine; and root beer required various combinations of spicewood, birch bark, sassafras, and prickly ash bark. Southerners also concocted an alcoholic beverage known as "cherry bounce" from the rum cherry.

By the Victorian era, the settlers had a greater amount of leisure time, which was reflected in their creation of cosmetics, many containing ingredients from the herbal grove. Oils of orange flowers, lemons, cassia, and cinnamon were used as hair treatments. Walnut bark and shells served as a brown hair dye. Both almond oil and paste were valued skin moisturizers.

Medicinal treatments also called upon herbal-tree offerings. An optimistically, but no doubt erroneously, named remedy known as James's Oil of Gladness (whose purpose now is indistinct) was made from hemlock oil. Myrrh was the secret of the tooth product George's Myrrhine. Today, myrrh is still used to promote dental health. Leg wounds were preferably treated with a plaster of elder leaves, but rotten apples could also do in a pinch.

Just as in Europe, the herbal tree was thought to have magical powers. Even through the last century, it wasn't uncommon to see "moonstruck," or ill, children treated by being coaxed through North American apple orchards or forests in the moonlight. Rowans and maples were plugged, wedged, and nailed with threads, ribbons, human hair, and clothing in hopes of transferring human diseases to them, and white oaks were split open to break a streak of bad luck. Not surprisingly, these practices often actually damaged the health of the tree. A recent, unfortunate instance reflecting the continuation of these beliefs in the healing strength of trees took place in Austin, Texas. There, the Treaty Oak, under which Stephen F. Austin signed a treaty with native tribes, was poisoned by someone attempting to transfer the power of the tree to himself. The tree is still living, but is now deformed.

It is true, trees *do* confer strength, but we needn't damage them to tap those powers. Their benefits can come to us in the form of fruits, nuts, bark, leaves, and flowers harvested and used in cooking, for healing, and as cosmetics.

Honey locust pods, like these grouped in a basket in a Southern garden, would have been harvested two hundred years ago for making a tea, now considered unsafe to consume. Before the days of readily available candy, children once ate the pulp inside the pods for its sweet taste.

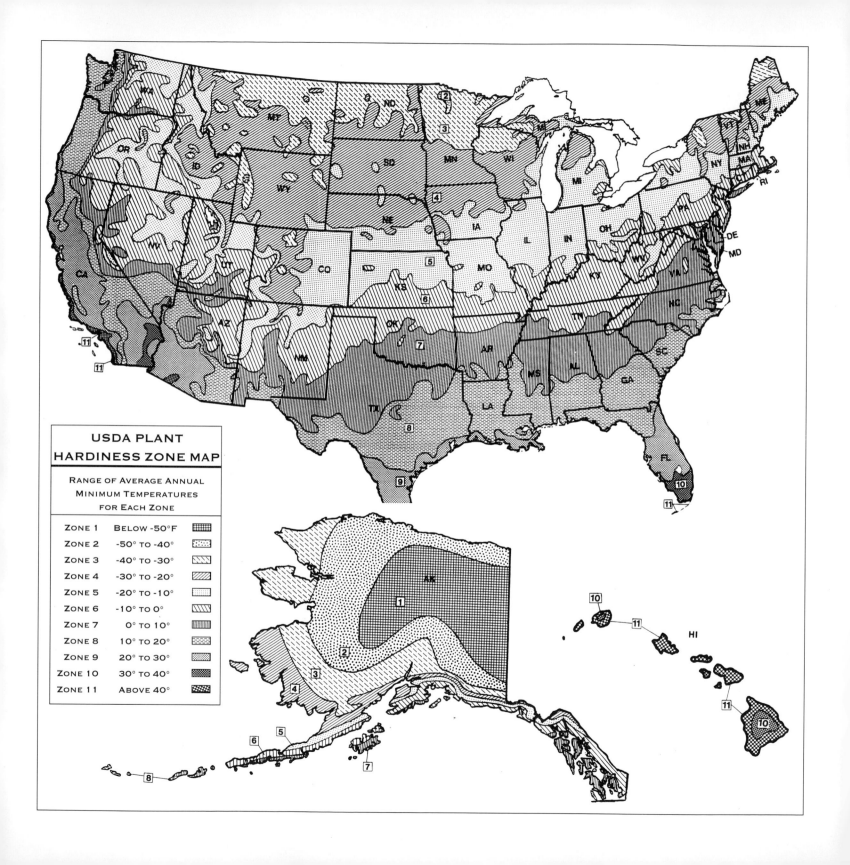

USDA PLANT
HARDINESS ZONE MAP

RANGE OF AVERAGE ANNUAL
MINIMUM TEMPERATURES
FOR EACH ZONE

ZONE 1	BELOW -50°F
ZONE 2	-50° TO -40°
ZONE 3	-40° TO -30°
ZONE 4	-30° TO -20°
ZONE 5	-20° TO -10°
ZONE 6	-10° TO 0°
ZONE 7	0° TO 10°
ZONE 8	10° TO 20°
ZONE 9	20° TO 30°
ZONE 10	30° TO 40°
ZONE 11	ABOVE 40°

TWO

CULTIVATING THE HERBAL GROVE

Many of the herbal trees mentioned in this book are common yard specimens. If you are beginning your own planting, keep in mind that you must select a tree that grows within your hardiness zone. Zones of plant growth given throughout the book are based upon the Plant Hardiness Zone Map of the United States Department of Agriculture, which appears on page 14. The lowest zone number given refers to the average minimum temperatures in which a tree will grow. Of course, microclimates often exist within given areas, so for very specific information on trees that will succeed in your area, consult with your local nursery or agricultural extension agent.

Make sure that the spot you select for your tree is well drained and that the soil has a pH that suits the tree. Most trees will grow in soils with a variety of pH, generally ranging from 5.5 to 7.0. Trees with special preferences are noted throughout. Ph is best checked by having a soil sample analyzed through your county extension service or by purchasing a soil test kit from a nursery. Ordinarily, trees require well-drained soils to grow. There are exceptions, such as willows, which will grow in more waterlogged conditions. The roots of all plants need oxygen in order to survive, so if you have an environment that's well drained, this helps get some air into the soil.

When deciding which trees to plant, keep in mind how large each one will grow and how far its branch scaffolding will spread throughout its lifetime. Again, planning like this will help you avoid future maintenance problems, such as the entangled branches of trees planted too closely together.

Balm of Gilead begins new life as a seedling. Like other poplars, it is a fast-growing tree sometimes used for reforestation.

How to plant

When you dig the hole to plant a tree, remember the general rule that the hole should be twice or even three times as wide and about as deep as the root ball. Most roots of trees develop within the top eighteen inches of soil, so the more lateral room you can give them the better. Don't plant the tree in a hole with equal distance down and across, as so many people do in error. The *wider* the hole, the better. Most trees are planted too deep. When you're placing the tree in the hole, keep it higher rather than lower. The root-crown area, where the top of the root system meets the trunk, should never be below ground. This way, the roots have access to air, which is crucial to their health. Never plant a tree deeper in its new home than it was in its native environment before it was transplanted.

Once in the ground, a newly planted tree should be watered. Thereafter, for at least a year, it will need a constant supply of water, about an inch a week, whether through natural means or through watering. It's important to get water to the *old* roots of the plant. Because the soil around the original root ball is less compact than the surrounding soil, water tends to flow down through the aerated soil area *around* the original root ball. To ensure that the plant gets moisture, build a shallow ring of soil around the planting hole. This will form a dike to retain water. Immediately fill the resulting basin with water. The dike should extend several inches beyond the original diameter of the root ball so that both old and new lateral roots get water.

Both commercial and home fruit-tree growers also make use of rootstocks, bases upon which specific varieties of trees are grafted. Rootstocks are generally available in semidwarf, drawf, and standard sizes and can, obviously, influence how tall a tree will grow or how much fruit it will bear. Some nurseries will custom-graft for you, so consult with them about these options.

When to plant

Spring and fall are excellent times for planting trees. A container-grown tree can be planted in either spring or fall, but the advantage of fall is that the plant will make roots throughout the cool growing season until the soil temperature

When leaves turn
colors in autumn, it's
a fine time to plant
container trees to
give them time to
develop roots
throughout the cool
growing season.

reaches 40 degrees Fahrenheit at the root zone, at which point the roots become dormant. The more time the plant has to grow, the more roots it will make, and the more established it will be by the time shoot growth occurs in the spring. When you plant in the spring, the tree has less time to make roots in its new home.

However, there is a danger involved in planting trees in the fall. Actually, it is not the planting but the *digging* around the roots that is dangerous. A way to avoid this is to plant containerized trees because the entire contents of the container—soil and all—is put in the ground. With this method you're not shocking the tree and it doesn't necessarily know it's been moved. However, there are certain plants that do not respond well to fall planting, even in containers. Among them are the stone fruits, such as peach and cherry, magnolias, and plants with fleshy root systems. If you're not sure when to plant a tree you have chosen, the best policy is to consult with a local nurseryman.

Balled-and-burlapped trees and bare-root trees are, of course, more fragile because the roots are more exposed than container-planted trees. These you may choose to plant in spring after the danger of frost has passed.

All container, bare-root, and balled-and-burlapped trees should be pruned so that the top growth of the tree is not so large that it overwhelms the root growth. Also, prune away any particularly scraggly or broken roots. Be very gentle when spreading out the roots of the tree in the hole; they are fragile at this stage.

If the so-called burlap on your balled-and-burlapped trees is a woven plastic, remove it after positioning the tree in the hole by carefully cutting it away so as not to harm the roots. If the burlap is organic, you can simply cut the ropes and leave it on so that it rots away naturally. Some nurserymen recommend backfilling the hole partway with soil after the balled-and-burlapped tree is in place so that the ball is supported prior to cutting the ropes; then tuck the burlap down and cover with soil.

In all cases, as you refill the hole, make sure the soil is firmly in place around the tree. Many professional arborists strongly advise using amended soil, not pure soil substitute or peat, but something that will serve as a transition between what's in the container or ball of earth and the ground around the newly planted tree. If you can, provide a half-and-half transition zone of site soil and container soil. Some nurseries, such as Hicks, recommend organic or bone-meal fertilizer. Again, consult with a local nursery or county extension agent to determine the specific fertilizer requirements for your region.

MAINTENANCE

Pruning is a necessary part of maintaining the health and vigor of trees. Although pruning helps determine the shape of a tree and can enhance its beauty, some people are obsessive pruners and tend to mar the beauty of trees in their earnestness. As you prune, keep in mind that your goal should be to remove only obviously dead or damaged branches. Use pruning tools or equipment geared to the size of the tree. Hat-racking, or pruning off the top of the tree, only makes it look ravaged and may even stunt the tree's growth.

The International Society of Arboriculture advocates pruning trees in winter or early spring. The society does point out, however, that there are certain trees you shouldn't prune at this time, such as the oak and the honey locust, which are particularly susceptible to disease in springtime. Therefore, it's essential to check with a reputable local nursery or your county extension service before pruning.

For those trees that have spring flowers, prune after the tree has bloomed. Pruning earlier eliminates buds that otherwise would burst into glorious spring flower. For those trees that bloom in summer the same principle applies. Prune anytime from the end of autumn to the beginning of spring, after you've enjoyed a season of bloom. Just be sure to prune before there are signs of new growth, which could be flowers in the bud.

Although the enthusiastic home gardener may wish to dabble in pruning, trees should be properly pruned by a competent, professional arborist on an average of once every three years.

PLANTING FROM SEED

If you fall in love with a particular tree, growing either on your property or in a neighbor's yard, you can try to cultivate offspring from seed. As with tree planting and maintenance, autumn and spring are both viable times to plant, depending on the species you prefer. It takes longer to grow a tree from seed, but it's also more economical than buying a tree from a nursery—especially if you have the patience to experiment or want to plant a large lot.

You can obtain reliable strains of tree seeds through nurseries or harvest them yourself. Some tree seeds, such as oak and maple, can be planted as soon as they mature. Others are more difficult to grow and require stratification, a process that imitates their normal dormancy or germination period. These seeds must be planted in the spring. But before they are planted, you must mix the seeds with moist sand or granulated peat moss in a sealed plastic or glass container and store them over the winter at a temperature just above freezing—35 to 41 degrees Fahrenheit—in a basement, garage, or second refrigerator set to this temperature. Before stratifying seeds, keep them in airtight containers at room temperature or cooler.

To plant seeds, whether freshly harvested or stratified, create a special nursery bed. Dig furrows $^1/_4$ to 1 inch deep, sow seeds thinly (4 inches apart), and cover with soil that has been mixed with organic fertilizer. You can carefully rake the soil into place. Water the beds. Once the seedlings have reached the size of a small plant, generally by the autumn after they have been planted, transplant them to the spot where you want them to grow. If you're reforesting a large lot, forgo the nursery bed and simply plant the seeds in the location where you want the trees to grow.

Specific details for trees that are easy to grow from seed are provided under individual entries. Complex stratification techniques are only for the experienced tree grower, and in many cases it's far more reliable simply to obtain a prestarted tree for planting.

Special Touches

There are a variety of wonderful, age-old techniques for pruning trees into special shapes. The classic espalier technique for fruit trees, by which a tree is trained into a branching shape, was very popular in France in the 1800s. It also became the craze in British manor gardens of the Victorian period, along with a number of other designs, including U or V shapes and criss-cross patterns.

One might also create a topiary or bonsai tree form in a container that can be moved to and from the garden. This is an art form that takes some patience. Good herbal-tree choices for these techniques include myrtle, bay, and the tea tree.

Herbal trees too fragile to grow year-round in the garden can be grown indoors. Those you might consider for this special treatment are the citrus, carob, bay, clove, coffee, fig, pomegranate, avocado, frankincense and myrrh (although the last two are quite difficult to acquire).

A remarkable New York–based organization known as the Rare Pit and Plant Council, or, simply, the Pits, is dedicated to educating people on growing and using indoor-grown trees and has very helpful recommendations on this subject. These people take on the challenge of getting a tree to grow from pits or seeds, although there are easier ways to grow trees indoors.

Here is the general procedure they advocate, using citrus as an example: Soak citrus seeds in water several hours before planting. Sow the seeds in a small pot filled with a moist, sterile medium, such as potting soil. Cover the pot with plastic to maintain a humid environment. Give the seeds some gentle bottom heat. This can be in the form of a fluorescent-light unit geared especially to plants, heating trays, or even by placing the seeds on top of the refrigerator. When seedlings appear with their first set of true leaves, usually within a month, begin removing the plastic gradually. First punch holes in it and then remove it completely. This will harden off the plants and not give them a shock. Move the plant to a warm, sunny place in your home and maintain a moist, but not soggy, soil. Don't put the new plants in a very heated location, however; just maintain a temperature of about 55 degrees Fahrenheit. As they grow, you can transplant them to larger containers. The secret of growing these plants is mov-

ing them along. Growth spurts occur about twice a year and this is when you should be ready to move them into larger pots. During the summertime, bring them outdoors to a warm location protected from wind.

Over the years, Pits members have grown dates from seeds, almonds from nuts, figs from seeds, pomegranates from pits, and even olives from pits. Growing olives from pits involves a particularly mind-boggling process that involves cracking the stone with a vise. If you have a container-grown pomegranate or fig tree, don't be alarmed if it drops its leaves. This is normal because they are deciduous. Just wait three weeks and the plants will be back to normal, with leaves and all. Remember, though, that a citrus grown from seed rarely bears fruit.

For those of us who would rather see fruit, another option is to buy a grafted tree, not a seedling, and, in colder weather, to keep it indoors in a south-facing window with relatively cool temperatures of 52 to 55 degrees Fahrenheit. You can use an 840-watt bulb to maintain the proper heat level. As with seed- and pit-grown trees, place grafted trees outdoors in warm weather.

GARDEN STYLES

Just like low-growing herb gardens with themes, the herbal grove can also be designed to evoke different moods and eras.

MEDIEVAL GARDEN

The herb garden of the Middle Ages was monastic and often walled, with fruit trees such as quince, hawthorn, and pear growing on south-facing walls. Orchards often surrounded the walls of such gardens. The pomegranate was a favorite in the medieval garden and is a significant tapestry motif of the period. To re-create this charming style, use small-scale herbal trees such as plum, callery pear, elder, peach, quince, sweet acacia, and Japanese persimmon (the last two mentioned grow in limited climates) as focal points. Surround these trees with such shade-tolerant herbs as violets, lemon balm, evening primrose, and sweet cicely. In other parts of the garden, cultivate neatly clipped raised beds of classic garden herbs such as mint, thyme, iris, clary sage, and calendula.

Grown in pots in a sunny courtyard, herbal trees can be a delight even when yard space is limited.

NATIVE AMERICAN PLANTING

Dogwood, honey locust, North American elderberry, sassafras, Carolina allspice, smooth and staghorn sumac, river birch, incense cedar, witch hazel, white pine, white ash, black walnut, Osage orange, and sourwood were all part of the Native American medicine chest. These trees look lovely grown alongside low-growing herbs used by native tribes, such as squaw vine and Indian nettle, or bee balm.

FRAGRANT GROVE

Sassafras, linden, Carolina allspice, magnolia, cherry, sweet fern, sourwood, Russian olive, sweet myrtle, elder, and Chinese chestnut all provide either fragrant flowers or foliage. In subtropical climates, add eucalyptus and citrus to this list of essential fragrant herbs. These trees are perfect planted around the perimeter of a scented herb garden full of the traditional roses, eau de cologne mint, apple-scented chamomile, and sweet rocket. Use smaller herbal trees such as myrtle and elder if you want to bring a vertical element to your scented herb garden.

CULINARY GROVE

Create a garden of edible delights by using any combination of apple, plum, cherry, walnut, persimmon, elderberry, and peach. Remember to make space allowances for each tree. Don't overlook such lesser-known trees as Chinese jujube, pawpaw, and pomegranate—which is a great deal hardier than most people think. Not only are the fruits and nuts of these trees delicious, but they are also used in many herbal remedies.

After a long, chill winter, ornamental trees blossoming in the grove have a magical quality. To enhance the allure of the scented springtime grove, add little stone basins of water to catch drifting blooms.

AUTUMN GARDEN

As autumn's chill sets in, red maple, flowering dogwood, scarlet oak, sassafras, and sourwood all add a pleasing scarlet color to any garden they're in.

If you would like some golden tones, add maple, persimmon, ginkgo, witch hazel, and fringe tree to your landscape plans. For colorful autumn berries, opt for hawthorn, rowan, and holly.

MAGIC GARDEN

Birch, sassafras, apple, witch hazel, oak, mountain ash, pine, and elder have all have been worshiped or have played a role in magic and folklore. Plant these and add magical touches to your garden with statues, reflecting balls, streamers, and wind chimes.

QUICK-GROWING GROVE

Sassafras, redbud, tree of heaven, willow, littleleaf linden, elm, and poplar (especially balm of Gilead) are fine arboreal choices if you want an herbal grove that provides immediate pleasure. Plant slower-growing favorites also, but have these trees on hand to make a lush garden that requires no patience.

POTTED TREES

Create a bed of traditional herbs by planting rosemary, thyme, and mint in a geometric plan with criss-crossed beds. At every juncture, place a potted tree. In warm weather, use bay, myrtle, the tea tree, frankincense, or the Italian-style pot-grown lemon. These can be moved indoors in winter and replaced by potted conifers.

Pruned into a fanciful swirl of shapes, this myrtle topiary would easily tuck into the corner of a city apartment. With sun and regular watering it makes a fine houseplant. Or use it in a container garden. From midsummer to autumn, the leaves are at the height of their spicy-sweet fragrance. This is the perfect time to harvest them; they dry beautifully for potpourri and make a fragrant insect repellent when tucked in a pretty cloth bag in a linen closet.

WILDCRAFTING AND THE HOME HARVEST

What you are harvesting from the herbal tree will usually determine when you harvest. Herbalists usually begin collecting bark in springtime and continue until the first days of summer. However, you should consult a reliable regional field guide that indicates when levels of bark toxicity, if any, are lowest. To avoid damaging the tree, remove bark from branches or twigs rather than the trunk. If you do take bark from a tree trunk, never remove a complete circle of bark. This can kill a tree. The inner bark of the tree acts as a conduit for nutrients, and so if a tree is girdled, the inner bark is also damaged and cannot transport food from the leaves to the roots. The tree will gradually waste away. Remember too that outer bark is a tree's first defense against disease. Certain types of fungi live on the outer bark of the tree and prevent other destructive types of fungi from entering. Removing bark encourages their spread, so do so judiciously.

Traditionally, a draw knife is used to remove bark. It is a sawlike D-shaped knife that is held with both hands on the curved handle. Just enough pressure should be put on the blade to create shavings, first of the outer bark, then of the inner bark.

Wild-harvested berries are another important ingredient in many of the recipes in this book. Sun-drying is an easy way to preserve mulberries, rowanberries, and wild cherries for year-round use. To do this, first wash the berries and depit the cherries. Some people "check" berry and cherry skins by dipping them in boiling water for thirty seconds and then immediately placing them in cold water. Others prefer simply to wash and depit cherries before drying them. After washing and checking them, spread the depitted cherries and berries out loosely on a raised screen or stretched cloth in full sun. Covering them with cheesecloth will help deter insects. Turn the fruit at least once a day so that it dries thoroughly on all sides, and bring the screen indoors at sunset. In the morning, place the screen outside again. The drying process may take two or more days. To check if fruit is dry, crush a few samples between your fingers: If you feel any moisture, give the fruit another day in the sun.

Some people like to pasteurize their dried harvest fruit to kill any possible contaminants. Dried wild cherries and berries can be eaten and cooked like raisins or reconstituted by soaking them in cold water for several hours.

When harvesting herbal bark from a tree, it's best to use a drawknife. Do not gouge the tree, but lightly remove shavings instead.

Whatever you choose to harvest from the wild, always know exactly what you are gathering. Take along a good field guide, preferably one with a regional focus. If you are unsure of what you've gathered, take it to a local herbalist or botanical garden for identification.

Don't gather plant materials on public lands. Be sure to notify private property owners if you are collecting fruit or other materials from their land. Above all, if harvesting from wild fields or woods, learn which plants are rare or threatened in your area. Dr. Barbara Duncan of Franklin, North Carolina, recommends following the Cherokee tradition of collecting plant materials only from the fourth tree of a particular kind you find. That way the species has a good chance of survival.

THE
HERBAL
TREES

MOST OF THE TREES NAMED HERE CAN EASILY BE CULTIVATED IN TEMPERATE CLIMATES. THEY GROW IN WOODLANDS, IN ABANDONED ORCHARDS, ON ROADSIDES, IN CLEARINGS, AND IN BACKYARDS. MANY TREES, SUCH AS THE BIRCH, APPLE, AND DOGWOOD, ARE WELL KNOWN BY SIGHT, BUT THEIR HERBAL USES AND RICH HISTORY SURPRISE MOST. OTHERS, SUCH AS FRANKINCENSE AND CITRUS, REQUIRE SPECIAL WARM-WEATHER GROWING CONDITIONS, BUT CAN BE ENJOYED FOR THE HERBAL BENEFITS THAT THEIR PREHARVESTED FRUITS, NUTS, AND OILS PROVIDE. AS NOTED IN CHAPTER 2, "CULTIVATING THE HERBAL GROVE," YOU MAY BE ABLE TO GROW EVEN THE MOST DELICATE SPECIMENS IN COLD CLIMATES IF YOU ARE WILLING TO PAMPER THEM INDOORS DURING THE WINTER.

USE THE PLANTING AND MAINTENANCE GUIDELINES FROM CHAPTER 2 TO PLANT THE TREES AND REFER TO SPECIFIC INFORMATION UNDER EACH TREE FOR PARTICULAR CONSIDERATIONS, SUCH AS SUN, SHADE, AND SOIL PREFERENCES.

On an old farmstead in the tobacco country of Tennessee, autumn olives line a pathway leading to a field. The fragrant little yellow flowers will eventually turn into nutritious, vibrant cardinal red fruits.

OBVIOUSLY, NOT EVERY HERBAL TREE IN EXISTENCE APPEARS IN THIS VOLUME. EUCALYPTUS, NEEM TREE, TEA TREE, INCENSE CEDAR, BALSAM FIR, TOOTHACHE TREE, LINDEN, QUINCE, SWEETGUM, WILD PLUM, WILLOW, REDBUD, HAWTHORN, SLIPPERY ELM, AND MANY TREES NOT PROFILED HERE HAVE HISTORIC OR CURRENTLY PRACTICED HERBAL APPLICATIONS. THIS SECTION CONTAINS A DIVERSE SELECTION OF FAVORITES THAT OFFER THE GREATEST RANGE OF BENEFITS FOR THE LAYPERSON. THE TREES ARE REFERRED TO BY THEIR BOTANICAL NAMES IN ORDER TO AVOID CONFUSION WITH THE VARIOUS REGIONAL NAMES TREES OFTEN HAVE. CULINARY, HOUSEHOLD, AND HEALING RECIPES FOLLOW MANY OF THE DESCRIPTIONS OF THE TREES, SO YOU CAN USE PRODUCTS FROM EACH TO THEIR FULLEST EXTENT.

SUGAR MAPLE, *Acer saccharum* RED MAPLE, *Acer rubrum*

Northern Indian tribes used to await impatiently their annual return to "sugar camp" in late winter, where they would gather in sugar-maple groves to tap syrup. Each camp was equipped with a comfortable sugar lodge where fires burned night and day to boil down the newly tapped syrup. Sugar camp was rather like an extended party, a time for hard work but also for storytelling and merriment. Tribes used the syrup to sweeten their simple, nourishing meals of fish, fruits, and cereals. Not only a luxury sweetener to the Indians, the syrup was also used as a type of cough medicine. A strengthening tea made from the inner sugar-maple bark was also a common cure among the Indians.

European settlers in North America quickly learned sugar tapping from the native peoples. Soon after their arrival in New England, colonists were tapping their own maple trees and drinking the sap, both for the pleasure of its sweetness and for its medicinal qualities. Maple syrup actually contains both calcium and iron and has been used in the treatment of these deficiencies. So, when we pour it on pancakes or use it to glaze meats, we are not only having a taste treat but giving our bodies a tonic boost as well.

The red maple has also been tapped for its sap, but the sugar maple is the best source for syrup sap. However, the sugar maple can't compete with the color that the red maple's boiled bark produces. It is an all-natural dark blue color that rivals the intensity of indigo.

Depending on where you were raised, you may have become acquainted with the maple tree in one of two ways. If your parents were superstitious and followed the customs practiced during the American Colonial days, they might have planted a maple tree when you were born to bestow you with a long life. Or, they might have simply passed you through the boughs of a mature tree to achieve the same end. But more likely than not, you learned about the maple

American settlers made a blue dye from the bark of red maple.

Even before the snow melts, these sugar maples will be tapped for syrup.

through your own exploration. Maple "helicopters" and false noses fashioned from winged maple fruits, also called samaras, are many youngsters' favorite natural playthings. As an adult, you may wish to use clusters of samaras in autumn flower arrangements. Because the clean leaves are so symmetrically defined, especially when pressed flat, they make wonderful stencils for the tops of cakes. Just sprinkle confectioners' sugar, cinnamon, or another spice around the leaf, remove, and serve.

The maple's leaves also delight us with their magnificent fall colors. The red maple's leaves turn a startling scarlet and vibrant yellow in autumn, while the sugar maple offers extravagant displays of orange, red, and gold.

To grow maples, give them a well-drained soil. They are not fussy about pH, are easily transplanted, and are fast growers. Both red maples and sugar maples thrive in zones 4 to 8. Maples are among the easiest trees to grow from seeds. When the samaras begin to ripen and fall from the tree in late summer, collect them and plant as described in Chapter 2.

Whether offering up a children's toy or adults' ingredient and medicine, the maple is one of the most statuesque and hearty residents of the herbal grove.

SWEET POTATO–STUFFED MAPLE PORK

The tartness of McIntosh apples combines with the sweetness of prunes and maple syrup to complement this festive pork roast, which could be served as the main course of a wonderful but nontraditional Thanksgiving or Christmas dinner.

2 medium-sized sweet potatoes
2 pounds center-cut pork loin, butterflied (your butcher can do this)
1 clove garlic, slivered
2 tablespoons salted butter
$\frac{1}{2}$ cup peeled, chopped McIntosh apple
2 teaspoons dried tarragon, or chopped fresh tarragon to taste
12 pitted prunes
6 strips bacon
$\frac{1}{3}$ to $\frac{1}{2}$ cup pure maple syrup
3 tablespoons apple cider or juice

As autumn days draw near, a dish of Sweet-Potato-stuffed Maple Pork makes a hearty feast.

Preheat oven to 350 degrees.

Bake the sweet potatoes for 35 minutes (this can also be done in a microwave, if desired), or until soft when pierced with a fork. Set aside to cool.

Trim any excess fat from the meat. Make random slits in the outside of the pork with the tip of a sharp knife and push a piece of garlic into each cut.

When the potatoes are cool enough to handle, remove and discard their skins and mash them with 1 tablespoon of butter. Melt the other tablespoon of butter in a small frying pan over medium-low heat. Add the apple and tarragon and sauté for about 5 minutes, stirring constantly, until the apple pieces are wilted. Mix into the mashed sweet potatoes.

Open the butterflied pork and place the prunes along the center line of the meat. Put the sweet potato mixture on top of the prunes and pat into a cylinder. Fold the two sides of the meat up over the filling and tie the roast around the center and at both ends. Place, cut side up, in a small roasting pan.

Wrap the bacon slices around the roast, tucking the ends underneath. Combine the maple syrup with the cider or juice and brush generously on the meat. Place the pork in the oven and roast for about 55 minutes, brushing on more of the maple glaze every 10 to 15 minutes. The meat is done when it reaches 170 degrees. (Be sure your meat thermometer is stuck into the meat, not the filling.)

Remove the roast from the oven and let it sit at room temperature for a few minutes before slicing. **SERVES 4 TO 6**

Naomi Black, author of *New England, Seashore Entertaining,* and other cookery books, contributed this recipe. See also Naomi's recipe for Apple Gingerbread on page 84.

SWEET OR SPICE BIRCH, *Betula lenta*

Under a cover of winter snow, white birch is one of the most poetic of all the trees. Venerated by Native Americans, the tree was a significant dream image.

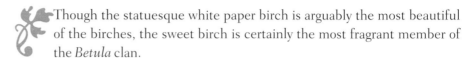Though the statuesque white paper birch is arguably the most beautiful of the birches, the sweet birch is certainly the most fragrant member of the *Betula* clan.

This unassuming species, with its gray or black bark, has provided us with a unique beverage: birch beer. Made from the tree's sap, birch beer was a great favorite in bygone centuries and was available as a bottled soft drink in the early twentieth century. At one time this beer was made with birch bark, prickly ash bark, oil of capsicum, grain alcohol, and other somewhat alarming ingredients. The Beverage Museum in Goodlettsville, Tennessee, displays an early-twentieth-century can of Queen-O-Royal birch beer, which guaranteed that its pure flavor came from "roots, herbs, and spices."

The bark, leaves, and twigs of sweet birch, or spice birch, as it is sometimes known, are pleasantly aromatic and smell like wintergreen. Some mountain people have chewed these minty twigs after meals to freshen their breath; they are a natural version of the minted toothpick or after-dinner mint.

Various parts of the sweet birch contain methyl salicylate, an analgesic. Native tribes made leaf and twig teas to soothe headaches and other pains. Perhaps this pain-relieving tradition inspired the practice often employed by early settlers of plugging the birch with sick people's hair or clothing to cure them of their ills.

Whether or not you feel under the weather, you could make a very pleasant, minty-tasting all-natural tea by steeping sweet birch twigs in water, straining it, and then adding some maple syrup or honey as a sweetener.

To add sweet birch to your grove, simply select a spot with acidic, well-drained soil. Not a temperamental tree, the sweet birch thrives in zones 4 to 8 and will

even grow in the shade. However, this tree is sensitive to transplanting, so springtime planting of balled-and-burlapped, *not* bare-root, trees offers the best results. If you want to try to grow the tree from seed, collect ripe catkins in late summer or early autumn when they are still green enough to hold their form. Shake the small, oval light brown or tan winged nuts into a bag. Plant the fresh seed in late summer or fall, according to specifications in Chapter 2.

Like its papery-barked relative, the sweet birch may not be a raving beauty, but it possesses the long-term, subtle winning ways of the girl-next-door. The sweet birch's oval leaves, pretty catkins, and innocent perfume give this herbal tree a charm all its own.

Found throughout eastern North America, sweet birch has a wintergreen taste and scent because it contains essence of methyl salicylate—once widely used to flavor soft drinks, candies, and medicine.

FRANKINCENSE, *Boswellia carterii*

Frankincense is such an exotic and sensual tree, even its name is a pleasure to say. Its elegant scent is both powerful and soothing, sweet but never cloying, and easily recognizable to those who have attended Catholic church services on holy days.

Many gods have been honored with frankincense smoke. The Greeks burned it to pay tribute to Zeus, the Egyptians to worship Ra, and the Chaldeans to honor Baal.

Only a truly remarkable tree could enjoy such widespread religious usage. In the third-century work *Deipnosophistai* (*Sophists at Table*), the Greek Archestratus speaks of frankincense and its haunting fragrance:

> *And always at the banquet crown your head*
> *With flowing wreaths of varied scent and hue,*
> *Culling the treasures of the happy earth;*
> *and steep your hair in rich and pungent odors,*
> *And all day long pour holy Frankincense*
> *and Myrrh, the fragrant fruit of Syria,*
> *on the slow slumb'ring ashes of the fire. . . .*

Many cultures have used frankincense outside religious services as well. The easygoing Babylonians used to anoint their bodies with it in lieu of bathing. Despite the great expense of importing frankincense, the ancient Egyptians used it prolifically: They combined it with myrrh and cinnamon bark in the honey pellets they burned to fumigate their homes; used it for embalming; scented their linens with frankincense smoke; and chewed it to perfume the breath (a complement to their dental-hygiene program of brushing with miswak [*Salvadora persica*] tree roots). They even thought it facilitated communication with the dead—a claim no contemporary air freshener could ever hope to match.

Small trees of Africa
and Arabia,
frankincense grow in
greenhouses when
given proper heat.

Workers make
incisions and
scrapings in
frankincense bark,
which releases
gummy emanations.
After these harden
into little crystals,
they are collected to
be used as incense.

Like good books with torn covers or old silver that needs polishing, this tree's charm does not lie on the surface. It has frondlike leaves with a somewhat curled, unruly appearance. Frankincense's bark peels away from the trunk easily and has a scaly look, but score the bark and it will emit a heavenly resin. It is difficult to obtain a frankincense tree for cultivation (though persistence pays off), and if you do get one, follow the information given under "Special Touches," page 21. Even if cultivating a frankincense tree is too demanding, you can be content to add the resinous "tears" to potpourri and incense blends to produce a scent that will transport you back through the centuries.

Spiced
HOLIDAY HERBS

You can easily adapt this deeply fragrant potpourri into an incense by powdering the mixture with a mortar and pestle and sprinkling it over hot incense charcoal to burn. If you are preparing this blend for the holidays, begin the process by mid-November. Most of the ingredients are available through potpourri sources. Because essential oils can sometimes create skin reactions, use of gloves is recommended. Vary the amount of each essential oil to create the fragrance you personally prefer.

$^1/_2$ cup dried eucalyptus leaves
$^1/_2$ cup dried sweet fern leaves (*Comptonia peregrina*), or sassafras leaves
$^1/_2$ cup dried desert sage
$^1/_2$ cup dried rose petals
$^1/_2$ cup sandalwood chips, crushed
$^1/_2$ cup frankincense

$^1/_2$ cup powdered benzoin gum
$^1/_4$ cup myrrh
$^1/_4$ cup powdered cinnamon
5 drops oil of pine
5 drops oil of sage
5 drops oil of cedar
5 drops oil of lemon
5 drops oil of lavender

In a large glass or plastic bowl, mix together all ingredients, except the oils, with a wooden spoon. Add the oils individually, drop by drop. Mix ingredients together thoroughly. Transfer the mixture to a glass or plastic container with a close-fitting lid and place in a cool, dark place for at least 3 weeks to cure. Stir from time to time. After the necessary amount of time has passed, display in a decorative bowl or several bowls. You can add whole dried blossoms of any flower or pine cones to the top of the fragrant mixture for a decorative effect.

THREE KINGS INCENSE

This incense gets its name from three principal ingredients: golden vetiver (a tropical grass with fragrant roots), frankincense, and myrrh—an adaptation of the gifts of the Magi. Because essential oils can sometimes create skin reactions, use gloves when preparing this.

2 tablespoons myrrh, ground
2 tablespoons frankincense, ground
$^1\!/_2$ ounce vetiver (*Vetiveria zizaniodes*)
10 drops oil of lemon
10 drops oil of patchouli

Curling tendrils of frankincense smoke wafted through ancient Egyptian temples and still create a magical aura at Western church services. Despite its sacred associations, however, frankincense is just as appropriate for home use.

Grind dry ingredients together with a mortar and pestle. Stir the oils through the dry ingredients with a wooden spoon. Transfer the mixture to a glass or plastic container with a close-fitting lid, and place it in a cool, dark place for at least 3 weeks to cure. Stir from time to time. After the necessary amount of time has passed, burn the incense by sprinkling it over hot incense charcoal, which is made from willow and available from incense suppliers. (Do not use charcoal briquettes.) A pleasant smoke will billow forth.

*Though its root and bark have been brewed
into a tea used as eye drops and a
treatment for malaria, Carolina allspice is
especially noteworthy for its beauty.*

CAROLINA ALLSPICE, *Calycanthus floridus*

Before the days of Chanel No. 5, young women preparing for the local spring dance would rush out into their gardens to pluck a branch of Carolina allspice, or sweet bubby, as they knew it. They would rub the flower on their wrists and behind their ears and would sometimes even place a sprig in their bosoms so that they could renew the heavenly scent throughout the evening.

Carolina allspice blossoms have a rich yet sweetly innocent bouquet. The flowers are of a pronounced dark red or purple color, with deep chocolate-brown undertones that give them an antiqued look. The inner petals form a graceful cup, while the outer ones tend to hang down in spidery wisps. Carolina allspice is especially prolific throughout the American South, as its name reveals, but it is also known as far north as Pennsylvania and into the Midwest (zones 4 to 9). Technically a shrub, Carolina allspice can easily grow to small tree size (about ten feet) if left to its own devices. It likes a rich soil, but doesn't take kindly to being waterlogged, so be sure the planting site is well drained.

In the contemporary herbal grove, Carolina allspice plays the role of fragrant dilettante, not performing any particularly useful function, but without question lending charm to its surroundings. Cherokee tribes were of a different opinion: They brewed the roots and bark as teas to soothe a variety of ills, and European settlers later drank similar teas to soothe jangled nerves. There is reason to believe that this practice is potentially harmful, so let us be content to sample only the fragrance of Carolina allspice. Certainly, the leaves, flowers, and bark are perfect for potpourri, but nothing could be more satisfying or spontaneous as creating a simple perfume in the manner of the bygone Southern belle.

Like a miniature corsage, the flowers of Carolina allspice are perfect with their burgundy-petaled finery and intoxicating fragrance.

CAROLINA ALLSPICE PERFUME CREAM

To make this beautifully scented cream, use a glass pint jar to make the liquid, and several sealable containers or one large 16-ounce one to store the finished cream in. You'll also need a double boiler or stainless steel bowl (keep in mind that these will be somewhat difficult to clean after use on account of the melted beeswax used in this recipe). The cream is especially effective when used on pulse points. People with allergies should rub only a small amount on a small portion of skin to test it.

6 ounces each flowers, leaves, and inner bark from Carolina allspice (enough to fill a glass pint jar), mixed, with leaves cut into strips and bark in small shavings
2 cups extra-virgin olive oil
4 ounces beeswax

Carolina allspice perfume cream brings an old-fashioned touch to the vanity table. Its simple, well-loved fragrance cannot be faithfully reproduced by perfumers using chemical substitutes.

Fill a clean pint jar with the plant material. Pour olive oil into jar. Shake the jar to make sure the plant material is covered and no air pockets remain. Let steep, covered, for 3 days.

Strain the plant material out of the oil. Pour the fragrant oil into the stainless steel bowl or double boiler. If you are using a bowl, put it in a pan of water to heat or place it directly over low heat on the stove.

Add the beeswax to the oil. Heat the mixture just enough to melt the beeswax.

Once the beeswax has melted, pour the mixture into the container(s) you want to keep the cream in and seal. Let cool for several hours. **YIELD: APPROXIMATELY 16 OUNCES**

North Carolina herbalist and folklorist Dr. Barbara Duncan contributed this recipe, which is sold by her company, Hearts o' Flowers. Other recipes from Barbara appear on pages 74 and 125.

CINNAMON, *Cinnamomum zeylanicum*

CAMPHOR TREE, *Cinnamomum camphora*

The trees of the *Cinnamomum* genus are among the most valuable and widely harvested in the herbal grove. Cinnamon and camphor trees provide us with spicy tastes, lovely scents for potpourri, and a soothing remedy for skin problems. These aromatic evergreen trees are close cousins in the Lauraceae family, which also contains the aromatic bay tree and the fresh-scented sassafras. Cinnamon trees are curious-looking, with a rather leathery bark, fragrant oval leaves, and small bluish fruit.

When we savor the taste of cinnamon, we are actually eating the dried inner bark of this tree's branches. True cinnamon sticks—not the candied kind—are delicate dried bark strips that twist into tendrils at the ends. Generally used in ground form, cinnamon brings a delightful lift to cookies and cakes and is especially wonderful with French toast, waffles, and sprinkled over fried breads. It is also versatile enough to flavor beans and squash, enhance pork glazes, blend with meat in Moroccan-style main-dish pies, and add a mellow spiciness to cooked fruits. Cinnamon is the key ingredient in a flavorful Arabian tea, is wonderful in cappuccino, and is essential in mulled wines. If all this were not enough, cinnamon-spiced liqueurs are not only delicious but are rumored to be aphrodisiacs. As with all aphrodisiacs, this is debatable, but the sparkling taste of cinnamon on the tongue certainly excites the taste buds.

Cinnamon also produces a wonderful aroma when used as an ingredient in autumnal potpourris. If you are looking for a particularly strong cinnamon scent, add a few drops of cinnamon oil instead of ground dry cinnamon to your mixture.

Although popular today, cinnamon was even more widely used in the past. For example, it was an important item in ancient Egyptian embalming mixtures and later was used in Victorian medicated waters and scented pomades.

The most valued part of the cinnamon tree is its hollow "quills" of inner bark, which is thoroughly dried to preserve its magnificent aroma. From May to August, the time of harvest, the aromatic sap is most abundant in the wood. Though Westerners think of cinnamon as a culinary ingredient, to the Chinese it is also a potent medicinal.

Cinnamon's close cousin, the camphor tree, is another herb known for its versatility. Camphor oil, a yellow resin found in the camphor tree, has antiseptic and soothing properties. In the past, camphor ice was a home remedy made by melting various oils and beeswax with camphor crystals, used to relieve skin irritations. Lavender oil and camphor were once combined to make a natural headache-relieving liniment. A type of liniment for colds known as camphorated oil was made with olive oil and camphor crystals.

Though you may want to rush out and buy *Cinnamomum zeylanicum* for your garden, remember that these trees are delicate and that home cultivation is limited by climate. Furthermore, harvesting the inner bark is a tricky business best left to the spice-trade experts. If you grow a cinnamon tree, the only thing you will reap is pride and possibly a conversation starter. In its native tropical climate, it can reach a height of thirty feet. This tree can be grown outdoors, with care, in the American South to zone 9. In outdoor planting, sandy loams suit this tree best. Indoors, cinnamon will thrive in a warm greenhouse-type room (See "Special Touches," page 21).

Not quite as fragile as the cinnamon tree, the camphor tree, a native of China and Japan, grows in Southern California, the Southwest, and the South, in zones 8 to 10. It likes a sandy loam but tolerates a variety of soils, as long as they aren't alkaline. It can grow to more than forty feet high, creating plenty of needed shade in these warm locales. Its glossy foliage and yellow flowers smell delightful and can be harvested for potpourri. When crushed, the leaves emit an even more intense aroma. It would be quite difficult for the novice to extract oil from a camphor tree, so settle for enjoying its interesting green-mottled bark and distinctive, head-clearing aroma.

*Mottled green bark
and a fresh scent
in the air are two easy
clues to identifying
the camphor tree.*

CITRON *Citrus medica* LEMON *Citrus limon* ORANGE *Citrus sinensis*

BERGAMOT ORANGE *Citrus bergamia* MANDARIN *Citrus nobilis deliciosa*

BITTER ORANGE *Citrus aurantium*

Precious few trees could claim to be more civilized than the citrus. They have always had rather regal associations. For example, they were cultivated in orangeries and limoniums in the courts of Louis XIV at Versailles and at Frederick V's castle in Heidelberg. During the reign of the House of Tudor, citrus trees were cultivated indoors in every proper estate garden. They were wheeled like languid royalty into the sunshine in balmy weather, so that a privileged few could feast on the fresh fruits.

With their highly aromatic blossoms, remarkably luscious fruits, and versatile peels, the citrus trees contribute to just about every herbal purpose imaginable. For centuries, they have been savored in every meal course, as fresh or cooked fruits or rinds. They are especially prevalent in Mediterranean desserts. Citrus fruits are also classic ingredients of marmalades, used to glaze everything from scones to game dishes. The essential oil from citrus peels and their deliciously scented flowers are used in cosmetics and perfumes.

THE CITRON TREE

Most people associate citrus plants with Spain, but that is not where the trees first grew. They are thought to have originated in tropical or subtropical Asia or Indo-Malaya. The first recorded citrusy trees were ancestors of today's citron, a short, spiny tree bearing yellow fruits with a very pleasantly scented skin, which is still candied to make commercial citron.

Invading Moors are believed to have brought the first orange species to Granada, Seville, and throughout Andalusia during the eighth century. The orange-blossom–strewn gardens of the Alhambra are fragrant reminders today of that invasion.

It wasn't until ten centuries later, however, that Spanish citrus began to be commercially cultivated, with Valencia as a central location. Today, deliciously scented groves dot the Mediterranean and, of course, Florida and parts of California. Citrus trees can also be cultivated, with care, at home in climates with cold winters if they are placed in a sunny window without too much heat and wheeled outdoors in summer to sit in a wind-protected spot (See "Special Touches," page 21, for citrus cultivation indoors).

Use the following recipe should you choose to cultivate citrus *and* you like to barbecue: When you prune off old citrus-tree branches, save and dry them for at least two weeks in a garage or basement. When it's time to barbecue, cut the dried wood into chunks, soak them in water for a half hour, and scatter the wood among the barbecue coals, lighting them so that they smoulder. The citrus wood will impart a slightly sweet, smoky taste that especially enhances the flavor of fish.

THE LEMON TREE

This charming tree, with beautifully scented white flowers splashed with pastel pink, usually grows about ten feet high in the orchard, but is much smaller in pot culture. Should you be lucky enough to obtain lemon flowers, dry them and add them to sachets, perhaps along with lemon peel. Sleep with the sachet under your pillowcase; this is thought to attract love, but, even if it fails, the scent will soothe you into gentle citrus slumber.

A vast Mediterranean citrus grove has been in continuous cultivation for three centuries. Though most often seen in large-scale plantings, these trees also make beguiling accent plants in the front yard.

For those who squander their savings on miracle cosmetics only to find the results mediocre at best, the humble lemon is an inexpensive, safe, and thoroughly delightful alternative. Drinking a glass of water mixed with the juice of a lemon will restore your skin's vitality by contributing to the formation of collagen, which maintains skin elasticity. Lemon juice's astringent qualities diminish troublesome teenage acne. Apply the juice lightly with a cotton ball at bedtime and allow it to dry overnight. Some people have had success whitening stained teeth with lemon juice. Many light-haired people who wish to highlight their hair have found that lemon juice does this effectively when combined with some sunshine, although the price is a dryer scalp. (This can be countered with almond oil, massaged through the hair.)

The vitamin C found in lemons helps to protect against flu and colds and actually has an energizing effect on the body. A home remedy for a cough or cold is to drink equal parts lemon juice and honey every few hours. Another lemon bonus is that the white inner rind contains vitamin C, bioflavonoids (which keep the walls of small blood vessels healthy), pectin (a form of soluble fiber, which helps lower blood cholesterol), and potassium (which regulates blood pressure).

Lemon juice is a wonderful disinfectant, which is why it is often squeezed on shellfish and other seafood that harbor bacteria. The juice is also a natural antiseptic and itch reliever for insect bites. We've known for centuries that lemons aid digestion. This is why a lemon sorbet is so soothing after a heavy meal. And essential oil derived from lemon peels is a key ingredient of Mediterranean liqueurs as well as many soaps.

THE ORANGE TREE

The finest-tasting oranges are those that have been subjected to a bit of frost. Just enough can make them extraordinary; too much can kill an entire crop. With this precarious existence, the orange is not always perfect, but when this classic fruit is properly ripened, it matches the most exquisite dessert for flavor.

Like the lemon, the orange gives us the natural gift of vitamin C. Herbally speaking, the orange is multitalented. Orange flower water, a classic European beauty concoction, acts as a toner for the skin. The peels of the common orange can be dried for use in potpourri and even in incense, for their evocative aroma. The orange's rather suggestive folk name, "love fruit," reveals its long-time link with romance, its having often been considered an aphrodisiac. The emollient quality of orange flowers makes them wonderful—and potentially romance-inducing—additions to bath mixtures that challenge the bather to, like the orange, live a bit dangerously.

THE MANDARIN TREE

In the West, the mandarin orange's readiness to shed its peel makes it a favorite of impatient fruit lovers. In the East, the ease with which the peel falls from the fruit is valued just the same, for to Chinese herbalists, the mandarin orange's rind is essential to regulating energy. (The Chinese believe that blocked energy can result from poor dietary habits.) The Chinese also consider the mandarin—along with the traditional orange—to be a sign of good luck.

The mandarin probably did not reach the European dinner table until the early nineteenth century, when it was first exported from China. It immediately became essential to the holiday table, due, in part, to the fact that the fruit appears in the markets at this time of year.

THE DELIGHTFUL DUO: BERGAMOT AND BITTER ORANGE

The bergamot and bitter orange are not readily available in the United States. The existence of these two somewhat eccentric species has contributed much to citrus's mysterious reputation.

Bergamot's essential oil is used for aromatherapy and perfumery; this spiny citrus is grown principally in Europe for its oil—not its pleasingly pear-shaped, though bitter, fruit.

The bitter, or Seville, orange has a remarkably fragrant flower and is indeed grown throughout Spain, where it is a prized ingredient in marmalade. Bitter oranges are so loved in Spain, especially as a seasoning, that Columbus carried them with him on his New World voyages—not necessarily as a precaution against scurvy but because he wanted to have a supply on hand in his new surroundings.

Versatile and vitamin-rich, citrus can be a daily part of our lives. Look beyond the fruits' obvious edible offerings, and you will discover a rich repertoire of uses.

LEMON ICEBOX PIE

On hot, humid summer days, it's a Southern tradition to sit back with a cool, fluffy slice of this special pie and a tall glass of minted iced tea. This recipe comes directly from the Deep South.

CRUST:
1½ cups graham cracker crumbs
1 teaspoon sugar
¼ cup butter, melted

FILLING AND MERINGUE:
3 eggs, separated
1 8-ounce can sweetened condensed milk
½ cup freshly squeezed lemon juice
Grated zest of 1 lemon
6 tablespoons sugar

Citrus is one of the most popular "dessert herbs." Lemons add tang and a delicate scent to the Icebox Pie pictured here.

Preheat oven to 350 degrees.

Stir together the graham cracker crumbs, teaspoon of sugar, and melted butter. Press into a 9-inch pie plate, being careful not to make the sides too thin. Chill at least 20 minutes.

Beat the egg yolks with the condensed milk until well blended. Stir in the lemon juice and zest and set aside.

In a separate bowl, beat the egg whites until foamy. Continue beating while gradually adding the sugar. Beat until the whites hold a stiff peak, but do not overbeat.

Pour the lemon filling into the chilled pie shell and spread the meringue on top. Bake for 15 minutes, or until a light golden brown. Cool completely on a wire rack, then chill well before serving. **SERVES 8**

Lynne Tolley, proprietress of Miss Mary Bobo's Boarding House of Lynchburg, Tennessee, contributed this recipe. See also the Lynchburg Peach Pie recipe on page 126.

SORBETTO AL LIMONE

Here is a classic summertime treat that is easy to prepare and remarkably refreshing to eat. Serve sorbet on its own or with fresh berries and a sprig of mint.

Juice of 4 large lemons
4 cups ice water
Superfine sugar to taste
1 tablespoon grated lemon zest
   (optional)

Combine the juice, water, and sugar to make lemonade, adjusting the sugar to taste. (Keep in mind that the colder a food is, the less sweet it tastes, so you should make the lemonade slightly sweeter than usual.) To intensify the flavor, add 1 tablespoon grated lemon zest.

Chill the mixture in the refrigerator for 15 minutes, then process it in an ice-cream maker according to the manufacturer's instructions. If an ice-cream maker is unavailable, freeze it in a shallow metal pan, stirring well to break up the crystals when it is about half frozen. Serve the sorbet before it freezes solid, or shave it with a knife after it is completely frozen. **SERVES 4 TO 6**

A few cooling spoonfuls of lemon sorbet following a meal is a traditional European method for aiding digestion.

Spanish Citrus Toast

French toast may be fabulous, but Spanish toast is splendid. Infused with fresh citrus, this dish is especially suited to brunch. Guests will even enjoy preparing their own.

2½ cups orange juice

4 eggs, beaten

1 cinnamon stick, cut into small pieces

Grated zest of 2 lemons (use lemon zester or fine cheese grater to remove)

Olive oil

1 loaf day-old peasant-type bread, cut into ½-inch slices

Sugar (granulated or confectioners')

Pure orange juice is more refreshing than carbonated soft drinks could ever be on a summer day and is a healthy ingredient in Spanish Citrus Toast.

Mix together the orange juice, eggs, cinnamon, and lemon zest and set aside for 10 minutes.

Pour olive oil into a large skillet to a depth of ¼ inch and heat over medium heat. Dip both sides of a slice of bread into the orange-juice mixture and place it in the hot oil, repeating with as many slices as will fit in the pan at one time. Fry on both sides until golden brown (about 3 minutes), keeping finished pieces warm until the entire loaf is used up. Dust both sides of each slice with sugar and serve hot. **SERVES 4**

This recipe comes from Alambique, a culinary school in Madrid whose head chef is Clara Maria Amezúa de Llamas. Alambique also generously contributed the recipe for Xato Sauce and Almond Cookies (see pages 118 and 119).

CITRUS SALAD

With a cold soup and some fresh bread, this salad makes a refreshing summer lunch.

8 large lettuce leaves (red leaf lettuce is best)
2 6½-ounce cans solid white tuna in olive oil, drained
4 oranges, peeled and sliced
4 hard-boiled eggs, sliced
½ cup black olives

2 scallions, chopped (white and green parts)
Salt and freshly ground black pepper to taste
Olive oil to taste
1 lemon, quartered

Place 2 lettuce leaves on each of 4 plates. Put one quarter of the tuna in the center of each plate and arrange the oranges and eggs around the fish. Top with olives and scallions and dress with salt and pepper, olive oil, and a generous squeeze of lemon juice. **SERVES 4**

Jannelle Wilkins of the Denver, Colorado, company Altamira Tours contributed this recipe.

CITRUS ORCHARD SOAK

This bath calls to mind the gardens of the Alhambra, which are redolent with citrus fruits, jasmine, and roses. All the botanicals used here should be dried. The orange flowers soften the skin.

2 tablespoons lemon peel
2 tablespoons orange flowers
2 tablespoons orange leaves and peel

2 tablespoons jasmine petals
2 tablespoons rose petals
5 drops oil of lemon *or* 2 teaspoons orange-flower water

Combine all ingredients, except for oil of lemon or orange-flower water, in a 1-quart pot and add enough boiling water to cover. Cover and set aside for at least 15 minutes. When ready to bathe, *strain* the liquid into a lovely bathing jug and pour this into the drawn bath in the old-fashioned manner. After the water has cooled slightly, add oil of lemon or orange flower water and distribute around the bath. Relax in this fragrant tub while sipping mineral water. **YIELD: 1 BATH**

DOGWOOD, *Cornus florida*

In southern England, until the nineteenth century, the leaves of *Cornus sanguinaria,* a close relative of *C. florida,* were a common cure for rabies, earning the tree the names houndberry and dogberry. These associations were transferred to the similar-looking *C. florida,* which became known here as dogwood. In the South, its dried bark has been used as a substitute for quinine, which is actually derived from the bark of cinchona, another herbal tree, to quell malarial fevers. Appalachians have also made a tonic for general debility by soaking the dried bark in boiling water. The bark has been proven to contain stimulants that boost circulation. In the nineteenth century, Hamilton's Tincture of Dogwood, a popular tonic, was made of dried dogwood bark that had been macerated in alcohol for two weeks. In addition, some Southerners even today will be able to show you how to use the peeled twigs of flowering dogwood as a natural toothbrush and tooth whitener.

Dogwood berries, which ripen to a glossy red along with the leaves of this tree in autumn, are also the base for healing tonics and are often sealed in brandy for just that purpose. The berries are quite bitter, however, and whether or not the tonic is actually beneficial has not yet been determined conclusively.

The leaves and berries of the dogwood are useful, but the flowers are what has earned it its fame throughout history. Actually, the showy snowy-white or pink petals so often associated with the coming of spring are not truly petals, but are the outer bracts that surround the dogwood's less-showy true flowers.

An old Southern legend says that the dogwood's flowers represent the crucifixion: The bracts form the cross, the notches on the bracts' edges the stigmata, and the greenish flowers contained within the bracts the crown of thorns. Perhaps this religious symbolism associated with the tree is what also inspired Appalachian peoples to carry about bits of dogwood petals and bark in small

Dogwood blooms
profusely in front of
a Tennessee
homestead. The
tree's bark, dried
and boiled, is an
old-fashioned
Southern tonic.

drawstring bags as protection from evil, in the same way that people today tote crystals.

A Cherokee legend explains the origin of the four large, notched bracts in a very different manner. The story centers on a man with four daughters who are constantly besieged by suitors. The father wants to capitalize on this attention, and so he instructs each of the suitors to bring valuable gifts each time they come courting. Eventually, the young men grow tired of this and seek less expensive women to woo. The daughters languish and begin to grow old. But the Great One intervenes, turning them into a lovely cluster of flowers, which reappear each spring for all to admire, free of charge.

Similarly beautiful, dogwoods native to other areas of the United States have also been used herbally. The berries of red osier dogwood (*C. stolonifera*) were eaten by various Western Indian tribes, who also used the bark and a decoction of the leaves to combat malaria. Western tribes sometimes combined animal fat and leaf or bark concoctions to make ointments. Chippewa Indians used the steeped root of the blue (or pagoda) dogwood, *C. alternifolia,* as an eye bath and also placed bits of the bark on their muskrat traps as charms to attract these animals. For pure enjoyment, this tribe also smoked the root of the green osier dogwood, *C. rugosa.*

The dogwood grows on other continents, where it also has herbal applications. In Chinese herbalism, the fruits of a native species of dogwood (*C. Kousa*) are prescribed for kidney and liver ailments. The fruits of the European Cornelian cherry (*C. mas*) have been used to make a sherbet and as a substitute for black or green olives.

Dogwood grows in zones 5 to 10 (the flowering dogwood preferring zone 5) and likes both dappled woodland shade and full sun. In addition to growing nurs-

Bordered by dogwoods, a country road sparkles with spring bloom. The white "petals" are actually the outer bracts of the plant; the less magnificent true flower is hidden inside.

ery-propagated dogwoods, you can try growing these trees from seed. Harvest the fruits in late summer or early autumn and plant them immediately in a garden bed, following instructions in Chapter 2. There is no need to extract seed from the fruit.

To keep your dogwoods looking wonderful, you should take steps to prevent dogwood anthracnose, a fungal disease that can strike the flowering dogwood and the Pacific dogwood (*C. Nuttallii*). This disease is not a threat to the Asiatic dogwood, *C. Kousa,* which is actually immune to it. The Horticultural Research Institute, based in Washington, D.C., reports that dogwood anthracnose has caused leaf blight, lower-limb dieback, and even tree death in dogwoods growing in forested areas since at least the 1970s. This fungal disease tends to strike forest dogwoods because they grow closer together than lawn specimens. So, to avoid the disease, plant dogwoods in well-drained, acidic soil in open areas that receive at least half a day of sunshine. Be careful not to inadvertently damage the tree trunk with a lawnmower or other mechanical device, which would make it more susceptible to disease. Don't *ever* replant a dogwood tree that was growing in the forest in your garden; always opt for a nursery-grown specimen. The forest transplant may be carrying anthracnose. When autumn causes the dogwood to shed its foliage, remove the leaves rather than using them in mulch. This will prevent the leaves from getting damp, thus preventing the opportunity for the disease to take hold.

If you take these simple precautions, your dogwoods should bloom beautifully each year, reminding you of the legend of the Cherokee sisters, maybe tempting you to explore Appalachian remedies, but always providing a tonic of natural beauty for the senses.

FIG, *Ficus carica*

The luscious fruit of the fig tree is really not a fruit at all. Beneath the dark purplish-brown or moss-green exterior, deep within the lipstick-pink or sunset-red pulp, bloom many Thumbelina-sized flowers. The only evidence we see of the mysterious workings of this millefiori world in which blossoms flourish in complete darkness, save for perhaps a ray of light entering through a tiny opening in the fig's outer flesh, are the tiny seeds that crunch when we eat this sensual fruit.

Herbally speaking, the furtive fig is an ingredient in numerous remedies, many of them time-honored in Europe. The fruit's success as a natural laxative is well known everywhere. An Old World prescription is made by macerating figs overnight in water, and in the morning eating the figs and drinking the water. Eating fresh figs is also prescribed in Europe for liver ailments. For stomach upset, many Europeans make a decoction of an ounce of dried, finely chopped figs. They simply simmer the chopped figs for fifteen minutes, add a spoonful of honey, and strain. Rinse and gargle with the warm mixture. For coughs, follow the same recipe, adding only a cup of milk and simmering for a little longer. After honey is added to the strained mixture, it's a soothing, warm drink.

If you want to enjoy the fig for its high nutrient content of vitamins A, B_1, B_2, and C, just incorporate it into your diet. The fruit is fresh on the market from June through late autumn.

The fig has always been an important food throughout the ages of Western civilization. Ancient Egyptians were fig eaters, but also employed the fruit for plasters and other medicinal treatments. Greeks of old used the leaves as a vessel in which to cook fish. Along with pears, plums, apricots, and cherries, the fig is one of the ingredients in Italian fruit mustard, a sauce used to spice meats. The French have always savored the fig for dessert, as do the English with their well-known figgy pudding.

One of the most ancient of fruits, figs were eaten by ancient Greek banqueters for their taste and by early Olympic athletes for stamina. Figs contain fiber, vitamins A, B, and C, and are not just for dessert—consider serving them cooked with pork or chicken dishes as well.

With its leaves lobed like a human hand and its gnarled stature, the fig tree has a dramatic presence.

If you live in the American South, the Southwest, or on the West Coast, you will probably be able to find a fig variety that will flourish in your garden. Figs are happiest in a zone 9 to 10 climate, yet have been known to tolerate cold up to zone 5, and have grown as far north as Michigan. Keep in mind that figs bear fruit on year-old and new wood, so prune during the dormant season to encourage new growth. The fig grows in a variety of soils, from sandy types to heavier clays. Even if you live in a region with chilly winters, you could grow the tree as a container plant (see "Special Touches," page 21) and bring it indoors during the colder weather. In fact, when cultivated indoors, the fig tree is said not only to bear fruit but to bring good fortune to the household. Remember, too, that the Buddha is said to have gained enlightenment under a fig tree—another excellent reason to have one around.

Healthy
FIG SHAKE

Based on a traditional European cure for an under-the-weather feeling, this delicious shake is as soothing as it is tasty.

6 whole fresh figs, coarsely
   chopped
4 ice cubes, cracked

1 cup plain yogurt
1 tablespoon honey
Wheat germ for garnish

Combine the ingredients in a blender or food processor and puree. Serve immediately, with wheat-germ garnish if desired. **SERVES 2**

Gɪɴᴋɢᴏ (ᴍᴀɪᴅᴇɴʜᴀɪʀ ᴛʀᴇᴇ), *Ginkgo biloba*

Long ago, when the earth was warmer, reptiles ruled, and the continents were going their separate ways, the ginkgo tree was firmly rooted all over the world. That was during the Jurassic period, 200 million years ago, and the quirky-looking ginkgo was perfectly at home among giant fernlike evergreens with leathery leaves and towering ancestors of horsetails that sprang up everywhere.

The Ice Age changed all that, reducing the ginkgo from its original landholdings in North America, Europe, and Asia to a modest retirement plot in China. By the time human civilization appeared, a mere ten thousand years ago, the ginkgo was still around. Its existence on earth today is due largely to the Chinese belief that it is a sacred tree, a belief based on its wealth of herbal offerings. Because the Chinese planted it in temple gardens and the Japanese later cultivated it with reverence, we are today able to admire this tree with prehistoric origins.

Struck by its unique beauty, plant hunters introduced the ginkgo to Europe in 1730, and it sailed to America in 1784. Lining city streets everywhere today, the ginkgo impresses with its imperviousness to pollution, having developed immunity to virtually every pest and disease possible over its long lifetime. It is particularly impressive in New York, where many ginkgo trees flourish despite poor soil and car fumes. Although it grows in just about any soil, the ginkgo prefers an acidic soil of 6 to 6.5 pH. It thrives on sunny sites in zone 5, but has been known to grow in zones as cold as 3 and as warm as 9. The fan-shaped leaves, which resemble the fronds of a maidenhair fern, inspired the ginkgo's other name, "maidenhair tree." The leaves turn a startling yellow in autumn and create a luxurious patterned carpet on the ground as they fall. The ginkgo leaf is so pleasingly shaped, in fact, that it was one of the most popular textile motifs of the American Arts and Crafts movement at the beginning of the twentieth century.

The ginkgo is more than an ornamental yard specimen; it is also a Chinese herbal mainstay. When its plumlike yellow fruits, which mature in autumn on female trees, are crushed, they have a foul odor that repels many people. However, Chinese herbalists collect them with the precision of pearl divers, for in their herbal repertoire, the fruits are highly valued. They are cooked or preserved for use as a digestive aid. In China and Japan, the pit's kernel is also eaten. Not only is it something of a delicacy, but it serves as an aid to digestion as well. Some people experience contact dermatitis from touching ginkgo fruit, so, just to be sure, take precautionary measures and wear gloves when handling it.

As reported by Steven Foster in his publication *Ginkgo* (see Bibliography, p. 157), the ginkgo leaf has been used in China for centuries to treat various conditions, including asthma and brain disorders. A tea made from the leaves is a common Asian medicinal beverage. Scientists are currently experimenting with these ancient applications and turning up promising results that may cause ginkgo to enter common herbal usage.

The ginkgo is the supreme survivor, having both made it through the Ice Age and made it in New York. Therefore, the ginkgo should be able to make it anywhere, perhaps with the exception of the Arctic and the tropics. The ginkgo is in no hurry to grow to its maximum size of one hundred feet. It will often take two decades for the tree to outgrow its "baby" branch scaffolding (the branches that give the tree an off-center, Picassoesque quality) and develop a full, rich crown. To encourage growth, give your ginkgo a little more water than other trees as it grows. You may find yourself dreaming of giant ferns and drifting continents, and of ripening fruit, perhaps being languidly munched on by dinosaurs.

A row of ginkgoes thrives on a Manhattan street. Trees are essential to maintaining a green element in an urban environment, removing pollutants from the air by storing carbon dioxide in their wood and returning oxygen for us to breathe.

WITCH HAZEL, *Hamamelis virginiana*

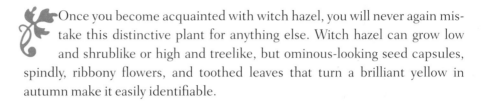

*Growing in umbrella
fashion in a forest
thicket, witch hazel
has a mysterious air.
Come autumn, its
wonderfully strange
flowers appear,
uncoiling in greenish
gold ribbon twists.*

Once you become acquainted with witch hazel, you will never again mistake this distinctive plant for anything else. Witch hazel can grow low and shrublike or high and treelike, but ominous-looking seed capsules, spindly, ribbony flowers, and toothed leaves that turn a brilliant yellow in autumn make it easily identifiable.

Common witch hazel is plentiful in the eastern half of North American and was a favorite medicine of native peoples. The Oneida tribe of New York State first used witch hazel for skin irritations. Today, everyone is familiar with the clear liquid witch hazel extract, which is distilled from the tree's bark, twigs, and leaves and used to take the itch out of insect bites, to soothe varicose veins, and as an astringent skin cleanser. Distilling witch hazel is no easy process, and considering how inexpensive and abundant the product is, it's best to buy it rather than make it at home. However, you can put your witch hazel to use in a footbath: Simply pour hot water over the fresh leaves, let them steep for fifteen minutes, then add the strained liquid to the footbath.

Growing witch hazel is a pleasure. To create an environment in which the plant will thrive, duplicate its woodland home in zones 4 to 8 by giving it moist, well-drained soil with a neutral to acidic pH and moderate to full sun. In the home grove, it does well with plenty of peat moss and compost and can grow to the height of a small tree, fifteen to twenty feet.

It's fascinating to watch witch hazel change with the seasons. In summer its bright green leaves and sheltering umbrella form make a verdant hideaway under which one can read a book or simply relax on warm days. The capsules that hang from the tree at this time resemble diminutive lanterns.

Come autumn, the witch hazel turns brilliant yellow. As the weather turns chilly, the capsules split open, and the seeds shoot out with a remarkable force

that can carry them as far as twenty feet. This odd trait strengthens witch hazel's ties to the black arts, for surely only a possessed plant could achieve such an odd feat. In fact, the witch hazel gets its name from the belief that its forked branches act as a divining rod to find witches. Some Early Americans also believed that witches used it to find gold. Forked branches of the tree were also used to find, or witch out, underground sources of water.

As you continue to observe witch hazel, the reason for the plant's other name, "winter bloom," will become clear. Its spidery yellow, sometimes orangy flowers bloom in a tangled web entirely out of synch with the rest of the plant world, from October to January. You'll have truly enjoyed your witch hazel to the fullest when you bring a flowering branch indoors to brighten your home when the weather outside is frightful.

When ripe, witch hazel nutlets eject their seeds long distances—an average of twenty feet. Perhaps such an odd habit accounts for the common name of the shrub or small tree, but more likely it had to do with settlers initially confusing it for European hazel, which was associated with sorcery. Nevertheless, witch hazel soon took on a magical reputation and was used by settlers for finding water.

BLACK WALNUT, *Juglans nigra* ENGLISH WALNUT, *Juglans regia*

Should you wander into the wilderness and come upon à towering stand of moss-clad black walnut trees, you might play archaeologist and search for signs of former human habitation. Known as dooryard trees, this native North American species was once a standard planting of the American homestead, for its nuts were considered invaluable for baking, its leaves and hulls were used as ingredients for medicines, and its wood was valued as timber and essential to veneer work.

The walnut made a valuable contribution to the medicine chest. If the bed bugs were biting, Colonial housewives might prepare an astringent walnut-leaf tea infusion to keep them at bay. Native Americans used walnut husks to combat skin afflictions, and Appalachian families borrowed this idea but added their own twist: They would combine walnut leaves and hulls with warm water to form a poultice and apply the mixture on a cloth to wounds. Pioneer families also found the walnut husk to be a very effective brown dye, as anyone whose hands have been stained from picking black walnuts knows.

Though the black walnut is a remarkable tree, the first American settlers might have been disappointed not to find their beloved English walnut growing on New World soil. This species had long been a delicious source of oil and nuts, and was also much used in medicine. Culpeper wrote of the tree, "The young green nuts taken before they are half ripe, is of excellent use to cool the heat of agues, being drunk an ounce or two at a time; as also to resist the infection of the plague. . . . The same also cooleth the heat of green wound and old ulcers." Currently, there are several European shampoos using walnut leaves to soften the hair. The hull is an ingredient in commercial buff face masks; using either the black or English walnut, try grinding the shell in a blender or food processor and combining the particles with a cleansing medium to polish the skin. Both walnuts also contain vitamins A, B, and C, as well as calcium, iron, phosphorous, and potassium.

Though they found the black walnut entirely to their satisfaction, certain American settlers must have missed the taste of the English walnut. This nut has a refined flavor and is more pleasing to look at, with its perfect symmetry, in contrast to the black walnut, which is irregularly shaped and has an earthier taste. The black walnut is also a harder nut to crack, but many believe it's worth the effort. Aside from baking with walnuts, try using them in soups and stuffings, adding them to meat and poultry dishes, and grinding them finely as an ingredient for sauces.

To ensure a fine flavor, grow walnuts yourself. Black and English walnuts can easily be cultivated together in the home orchard. Most walnut varieties need no pollinator, but double-check with your nursery to ensure that the type you select is self-fruitful. Black walnuts excel in zones 4 to 8, English walnuts in zones 4 to 6. Walnuts require little maintenance, perhaps a bit of pruning during the dormant season. Plant high-quality seedlings, give them a rich, well-drained soil, and you may be shaking walnuts from your grove and putting your industrial-strength nutcracker to work in five years or less!

WALNUT LEAF SACHET

This aromatic sachet deters moths from woolens and linens and keeps insects away in general. In fact, a folk usage of walnut leaves is to rub them on one's arms and legs as a bug repellent.

$^1/_3$ **cup dried walnut leaves, crushed**

$^1/_3$ **cup dried rue (*Ruta graveolens*) leaves or dried pennyroyal leaves, crushed**

$^1/_3$ **cup dried yarrow (*Achillea millefolium*) leaves, crushed**

Mix ingredients in a bowl and add them to a drawstring sachet bag to hang in a closet or sew them into a small pillow to tuck into drawers.

Clusters of black walnuts ripen in autumn. They are wonderful added to breads, cakes, stuffings, and casseroles. Native Americans once chewed black walnut bark to relieve toothaches.

WALNUT–WHEAT BERRY SALAD

Here is a versatile, healthy, and satisfying salad that can be varied endlessly depending on the ingredients you have on hand. It is particularly tantalizing and tasty if you add black walnuts harvested from the home orchard. This recipe is enough to serve a small crowd; it's fun to put all the ingredients out separately and let your guests mix their own salads.

1 pound wheat berries
1 cup chopped walnuts

ANY OR ALL OF THE FOLLOWING, TO TASTE:
Thinly sliced red onion
Chopped scallions
Julienned orange zest
Golden raisins
Chopped parsley
Chopped mint
Pomegranate seeds
Salt and freshly ground black
**   pepper to taste**

DRESSING:
Walnut oil
Vegetable oil
Raspberry vinegar

Cook the wheat berries by boiling in salted water until tender (this may take 2 hours or longer, depending on the type and condition of the wheat). Drain and cool to room temperature. Mix in the chopped walnuts.

Whisk the dressing ingredients together, using one part each of walnut oil, vegetable oil, and vinegar.

Mix the salad ingredients together as desired, season with salt and pepper to taste, and toss with the dressing.

Joel Jason of the New York catering company In Your Kitchen shared this recipe. Turn to page 133 for Joel's other contribution, Orange Chicken Breasts with Pomegranate.

The earthy taste of black walnuts enlivens Walnut–Wheat Berry Salad. Wheat berries are whole wheat kernels with a nutty flavor that enhances the walnuts' taste.

BLACK WALNUT CAKE

Black walnuts are plentiful in autumn, when Barbara Duncan's mother, Maxine Reimensnyder, used to gather them in the hills of Pennsylvania for her spectacular Black Walnut Cake.

2 cups butter, softened
2 cups firmly packed dark brown
  sugar
3 eggs, separated
2 cups flour
3 teaspoons baking powder
$^1/_2$ teaspoon salt

$^2/_3$ cup milk
1 teaspoon vanilla
1 cup black walnuts, finely
  chopped (not ground)
White Butter Frosting (recipe
  follows)

Preheat oven to 250 degrees.

Cream the butter and sugar together. Add the egg yolks, one at a time, beating well after each addition.

Sift together the dry ingredients and add to the egg mixture. Stir in the milk and vanilla. Beat the egg whites to soft peaks and fold into the batter. Gently fold in the walnuts.

Bake for 1 hour and 10 minutes in 2 greased 8-inch round layer pans or one 13- by 9-inch pan. Remove from the oven and cool completely on wire racks. Frost with White Butter Frosting. **SERVES 8 TO 10**

WHITE BUTTER FROSTING

1 pound confectioners' sugar,
  sifted
$^1/_2$ cup butter, softened

Dash salt
1 teaspoon vanilla
Milk

Beat sugar, butter, salt, and vanilla together with an electric mixer. Add milk 1 tablespoon at a time and continue beating until frosting is creamy and spreadable.

North Carolina herbalist and folklorist Barbara Duncan, Ph.D., contributed this recipe, passed down from her mother, Maxine Reimensnyder.

BAY TREE, *Laurus nobilis*

Our years spent toiling in undergraduate school are rewarded with the baccalaureate degree, a reference to the former practice of crowning medical scholars with berried laurel garlands, or *bacca lauri*. And our poet laureates are so named for the old Greek and, later, Roman custom of crowning athletic and scholarly champions with laurel wreaths.

These practices were inspired by the Greek myth of the sun god Apollo and the nymph Daphne. Apollo pursued Daphne so persistently that she turned herself into a bay tree to thwart his advances. To mourn the demise of the human form of his love, Apollo entwined a chaplet of leaves in his hair to demonstrate his sorrow and to send a clear message to mortals that the tree was divine.

Perhaps the myth has a subtext, for it could well be that as flesh and blood, Daphne wasn't able to bear the intense heat of Apollo, but as the sun-worshiping bay tree, she was able to receive his advances with pleasure. The bay tree originated in Asia Minor and the Mediterranean, where it enjoys lavish sunlight that can coax it to heights of sixty feet. In areas with merciful winters, such as Southern California and Florida (zones 8 to 11), it will flourish outdoors year-round in ordinary soil and may grow as high as ten feet or more. In other areas, bay is best grown in pots and moved indoors for winter (see "Special Touches," page 21). It won't grow as high, of course, but it makes a sculpturelike accent in the garden. One enterprising British couple sinks potted bays into custom-dug holes on their property to achieve the look of landscaped trees. Once brought indoors, the bay tree, being an evergreen, can ornament the home year-round and looks especially lovely in a round, topiary shape. It lends a bit of classical dignity to even the most unglamorous surroundings.

There are many reasons to grow a bay tree. A single dried bay leaf can flavor vinegar and bring a wonderfully spicy taste to stews, sauces, and marinades. Remember to remove it before serving a seasoned dish, however, to avoid

Bay standards flank a doorway, lending a classical elegance in their symmetry. Once chilly weather sets in, they'll be brought into a sunny spot in the kitchen so that their leaves can readily be used for stews, sauces, and fish stocks.

painful surprises. Dried bay leaves, burned among barbecue coals, give grilled foods a pleasant spiciness. Bay also makes a soothing bath herb. To make a bath mixture, infuse several leaves by pouring boiling water onto them and letting them steep for at least fifteen minutes, then add the strained liquid to the bath. And for those who dabble in the more esoteric realm of herbalism, the presence of this most esteemed and honorable tree in the home is thought to protect you from lightning, sorcery, and any other malevolent elements.

SPICY GREEK-STYLE STEW

Redolent of wine, garlic, and spices, here is the perfect stew to prepare in advance and serve for lunch when weekend houseguests arrive. You need only pluck a single bay leaf from your prized topiary (or your spice rack) to make this aromatic dish.

3 pounds beef stew meat, cut into $^1/_2$-inch cubes
Salt and pepper to taste
$^1/_2$ cup butter
$2^1/_2$ pounds onions, coarsely chopped
1 6-ounce can tomato paste
$^1/_3$ cup red wine

2 tablespoons herb vinegar
1 tablespoon dark brown sugar
1 clove garlic, minced
1 bay leaf
1 cinnamon stick
$^1/_2$ teaspoon whole cloves
2 tablespoons raisins

Season the meat with salt and pepper. Melt the butter in a large, heavy pan over medium heat. Add the meat and brown well on all sides. Cover with the onions. Mix the remaining ingredients together and pour over the meat and onions. Cover and simmer 3 hours without stirring. **SERVES 8 TO 10**

Louise Hyde of Well-Sweep Herb Farm in Port Murray, New Jersey, contributed this recipe.

OSAGE ORANGE, *Maclura pomifera*

Many people's first encounter with the Osage orange is a rather unsettling one. Coming upon the acid green fruits scattered about the ground, their "brain tissue" exteriors sprouting tiny hairs, one might believe that extraterrestrials had been engaged in a game of boccie ball. Upon closer inspection, it becomes clear that the fruits were dropped from the nearby tree with an orange-brown bark. Reach into the tree for an "orange," and you may receive a second shock, a sharp dig from the spiny branches.

Originally a plant of cattle country in the middle and southwestern United States, the Osage orange now grows throughout the country. Pioneers first used it as a livestock barrier and windbreak. This is because it can be trained into a very dense and spiny hedge. The practice inspired the tree's common name, "hedge apple"; another nickname, "horse apple," grew out of equine appreciation of the fruits. The wood of Osage orange has been used to create a golden-yellow or orange dye.

Urbanites have discovered an effective use for this unusual tree. They use its "oranges," which are actually inedible, as a cockroach repellent. They are most effective when sliced up and placed unobtrusively in pest-ridden places, such as kitchens and baths. They have a rather refreshing, clean fragrance, somewhat like that of apples. Some people have an adverse reaction to the fruit's milky sap, the bloodline it shares with other mulberry family members, so wear gloves when handling Osage oranges. Harvest the fruits in late summer and autumn.

The Osage orange is easy to grow and will flourish even in a poor soil. Originally a resident of the Plains and the Southwest, it now grows throughout America in zones 5 to 8, from the Northeast to the Southwest, through the Midwest, and even in Washington and Oregon. Growing the Osage orange from seed is messy but usually successful. To do so, collect fruits in late sum-

Osage orange fruits are easily camouflaged in autumn. However, when they fall to the ground, their bright green colors immediately catch the eye. The tree's wood yields an orange-yellow dye.

mer and throughout autumn. Keep them in a pile in the garage or outdoors for the entire winter. By springtime they will be mushy. Macerate the fruits with a rolling pin. Then, wearing gloves, extract the seeds from the fruit. Plant the seeds after the danger of frost has passed, following instructions in Chapter 2. Alternatively, to increase the odds of germination, stratify the seeds for thirty days, at 41 degrees Fahrenheit, following instructions in Chapter 2. Of course, you could always just plant a nursery-grown tree.

Once you get used to it, you may look upon the Osage orange as a thing of beauty. Give it time. Like Bergman films and escargot, this spiky, green-fruited tree is most certainly an acquired taste.

OSAGE ORANGE HOME REMEDY

Pick "ripe" Osage oranges in autumn, after the fruit has turned a bright green-yellow. If you pick it from the tree, be sure to avoid thorns. From the ground, select fruit that has no brown spots and has not already split open.

Stacked in a bowl in the kitchen, osage orange fruits exude their peculiar fresh scent, an effective pest deterrent.

Place fruits in your kitchen, bath, or anywhere else where roaches or other insects proliferate. For best results, split open the fruit and use its sections. Take care not to get any juice on your hands, as it is an irritatant to some people's skin.

APPLE, *Maclura pumila*

The ancient apple is our earthly symbol of paradise. Some people believe it was the tree of knowledge in the garden of Eden. In Celtic mythology, Avalon is characterized as the Isle of Apples, an idyllic place where the weather is always perfect. Norse mythology holds that the "Great Mother" takes earthly form as an apple tree and whoever eats her fruit might also become divine.

The amorous apple has always been considered a food of love. It was Venus's favorite fruit, and it is said that the simple act of splitting an apple with the object of your affections will ensure a lifelong love affair. This sensual fruit is available to eat year-round because of its long shelf life. The apple contains various minerals, vitamin E, and digestive enzymes. Its juice helps purify the body as the broad variety of nutrients strengthens the blood, and a healthful tea made from the dried peel is thought to ease muscle and joint stiffness. The peel contains pectin, which supplies galacturonic acid, a toxin eliminator. Today it is essential to use organically grown apples for teas in order to avoid ingesting harmful pesticides that are commonly sprayed on many commercially harvested ones.

Take advantage of the apple's healthful benefits by preparing dishes containing this fruit year-round. You can sample a wide range of textures, tastes, and colors with the many varieties of apples: the diminutive lady apple, the crisp Granny Smith, the tangy McIntosh, the juicy yellow Mutsu, and the antique Newton pippin. Apple appreciators find their own favorite ways to use them. Historically, Scandinavians enjoy cool summer apple soup with blue cheese, Appalachian-dwelling Americans dote on apple butter, Austrians liberally douse apple vinegars, and the French enjoy *pommes reinettes au miel et beurre salé* (fresh apple with honey and salted butter) and *pommes bonne femme* (cooked sugared apples).

Visit apple orchards at harvest time and you will be astounded by the many varieties—over two thousand in the United States alone. In addition to being delicious to eat, apples contain pectin and fiber. Pectin performs several vital functions: it eliminates toxins, stimulates digestion, and helps balance cholesterol levels.

Although apples are really a northern fruit, some types will grow quite nicely in warm, but not desert or tropical, areas, of zones 2 to 8. When planting apples, be sure to plant at least two varieties so that the trees will be cross-pollinated and set fruit; your nursery can advise you on specifics. If you're a gifted gardener, try training an apple tree into a regal espalier form; if you are not yet an expert you can find a nursery that will pretrain the tree for you. Apples like the warmth of the sun and enjoy a well-drained soil mixed with peat. They can ripen anytime from September to November, usually within the first three years of planting. For best results, prune the tree during the dormant stage to create a cup shape. The little nodule that extends from the branch and holds the apple is called a spur. Spurs bear fruit for a decade or more, so be sure not to inadvertently pull them off when picking apples.

Take the pruned branches, place them in the garage to let them dry, and use them either alone or in combination with coals on your grill. Before grilling, soak the branches in water for a half hour so that they will smoulder rather than flare, then add the wood chunks to the hot coals. They will bring a mild and sweet taste to poultry, vegetables, and anything else you might grill.

True romantics also plant apples for their fluttery spring flowers, which can be added to love-potion potpourris along with other herbs of love, such as rose, orange, violet, and sweet pea blossoms. Placed in a decorative bedside bowl or added to a sachet tucked under your pillow, such fragrant mixtures are said to conjure Venus herself, the ultimate guardian of the apple.

JUICE JULEP

Here are several fruits of the herbal grove combined to make a delicious summer cooler. Add a splash of rum for a terrific cocktail.

1 quart chilled unsweetened apple juice
1 cup chilled unsweetened pineapple juice

1 cup chilled orange juice
¹/₄ cup chilled lemon juice
Mint sprigs for garnish

Combine apple, pineapple, orange, and lemon juices in a 2-quart pitcher. Mix well and serve in tall glasses filled with ice cubes. Garnish each glass with a sprig of mint. **MAKES ABOUT 1¹/₂ QUARTS**

APPLE FRITTERS

A novel alternative to apple pie, fritters also work beautifully as a casual appetizer to a meal. Dust the hot fritters with a bit of confectioners' sugar or cinnamon to dress them up.

$1/2$ cup milk
1 egg
2 tablespoons butter or margarine, melted
Juice and grated zest of $1/2$ orange
$1/2$ cup chopped apples (skin can be left on)
$1/2$ teaspoon vanilla
$1\,1/2$ cups cake flour
$1/4$ teaspoon salt
$1/2$ cup sugar
1 tablespoon baking powder
Vegetable oil

The next time you're left with a few stray apples that are not quite enough to make applesauce or a pie, concoct Apple Fritters instead. They're especially nice served with apple butter, which unlike real butter, contains no fat.

In a large bowl, combine milk, egg, butter or margarine, orange juice and zest, apples, and vanilla. Sift together cake flour, salt, sugar, and baking powder in a separate bowl. Stir the dry ingredients into the milk mixture with a spoon, just until blended.

Pour oil into a large frying pan to a depth of $1/2$ inch and heat over medium-high heat to just below the smoking point. Drop batter by large spoonfuls into the hot oil (don't crowd the pan). Fry on both sides to a golden brown. Drain on paper towels and serve hot. **MAKES ABOUT 24 FRITTERS**

Applewood Farmhouse Restaurant of Sevierville, Tennessee, makes these delicious fritters from apples grown in adjacent orchards. This mecca for apple aficionados also contributed the Juice Julep recipe on the preceding page.

APPLE GINGERBREAD

Here is a new twist on gingerbread, an old favorite. The apple adds a delightful contrast in flavor and texture.

1¹/₂ cups flour
1 teaspoon baking soda
¹/₂ teaspoon salt
1 teaspoon ground ginger
¹/₂ teaspoon ground allspice
¹/₄ teaspoon ground cloves
Pinch nutmeg
Pinch cardamom
¹/₂ cup butter, softened
¹/₄ cup firmly packed light brown sugar
¹/₄ cup firmly packed dark brown sugar
2 eggs at room temperature
2 tablespoons plus 1 teaspoon molasses
¹/₂ cup milk
1 large apple, peeled, cored, and coarsely chopped
Confectioners' sugar for garnish
Whipped cream for garnish

Decorated with "stencils" of cleaned maple leaves, Apple Gingerbread is a comforting winter dessert—especially delicious served with fresh whipped cream. When sliced, little chunks of fruit sparkle inside.

Preheat oven to 350 degrees. Butter and flour an 8-inch round cake pan and set aside.

Sift together the flour, baking soda, salt, and spices and set aside. In a large bowl, cream the butter and light and dark brown sugars with an electric mixer. Beat in the eggs, one at a time, add the molasses, and beat well. Add the flour mixture in thirds, alternating with the milk, beating after each addition. (The batter will be lumpy.)

Pour the batter into the prepared pan. Scatter the chopped apple on the batter and push the pieces down until they are almost covered.

Bake for 35 minutes and test with a cake tester or toothpick. If the tester does not come out clean, bake for another 5 minutes. Remove the gingerbread from the oven, loosen the sides with a knife, and cool completely on a wire rack. To decorate, place a doily or some flat leaves on top of the cake and sift confectioners' sugar over them to create a pattern. Remove the doily or leaves and serve the gingerbread with whipped cream, if desired. **SERVES 8**

Naomi Black, author of *Seashore Entertaining* and other cookery books, contributed this recipe. See Naomi's other recipe, for Sweet Potato–stuffed Maple Pork, on page 35.

TART APPLE TEA

Apples have long been famous for their medicinal properties. This easy-to-make tea is an old Victorian recipe that was used to ward off illness. If you feel like you have a cold coming on or are a bit under the weather, give it a try. It's a good way to use up slightly bruised but otherwise perfectly good apples.

5 tart apples, peeled, cored, and sliced

Honey to taste (optional)

Bring 2 pints of spring water to a boil. Add apples and boil, covered, for 10 minutes. Remove from heat and let cool to room temperature. Strain and drink, sweetened with honey, if desired. **MAKES ABOUT 4 CUPS**

APPLE BUTTER

Here is a sweet, lightly spiced version of a Colonial American classic, which makes it possible to enjoy fall's bounty of apples year-round.

4 pounds tart apples

4 to 5 cups sugar

1 teaspoon ground cloves

1 teaspoon ground cinnamon

½ teaspoon ground allspice

Wash the apples, cut them into quarters (don't remove the cores or skin), and place them in a large stainless steel or enamel saucepan with 2 cups of water. Cover the pot and simmer the apples on low heat until very tender, about 30 minutes. Remove from the heat and force the apples through a sieve, discarding the skins and seeds. Measure the puree (there should be about 10 cups), return it to the pan, and add half as much sugar. Stir in the spices. Place the saucepan over very low heat and simmer for about 2 hours, stirring frequently, until the butter is very thick. (A heat diffuser or asbestos mat under the pot is very helpful—the butter burns quite easily.) Pour into sterilized 8-ounce jars and seal with sterilized 2-piece lids. **MAKES ABOUT 5 PINTS**

RED MULBERRY, *Morus rubra* WHITE MULBERRY, *Morus alba*

Mulberries, the prized trees of our great-grandparents, have been overlooked in recent times. In the not-so-distant past, the purplish-red fruits of the native red mulberry were often used in wine-making and were widely enjoyed in preserves. The berries were great favorites of Victorian children, who popped them lazily into their mouths on summer afternoons, along with ripening blackberries and raspberries, which they much resemble.

Today, many people believe mulberries are too sweet and leave them to over-ripen on the tree, a welcome feast for birds and even cattle. But these fruits offer a natural dose of vitamin C and can be baked into pies, used like blueberries in sauces for duck or game, baked into muffins and breads, or simply eaten fresh with cream.

The mulberry also boasts an impressive herbal résumé. Native American tribes used the juice of mulberry leaves and stems to treat ringworm externally. European pioneers powdered the bark and used small amounts as a laxative.

Perhaps the red mulberry fell into disuse because it's a messy tree, staining everything below it a deep crimson as it drops its juicy summer berries. This sloppy habit might also have inspired the folk belief that the sanguine berries are red with human blood, stored by witches on the tree until they turn black with ripeness. Perhaps another source of this belief is the fact that unripe mulberry fruits are said to cause hallucinations. To avoid these complications, pick the fruits only when they have turned a deep purplish red at the height of summer and have begun to fall to the ground. Don't plant the tree near pavement or other nongrassy areas that could become stained with berries.

No one could pin the same Draculean reputation on the white mulberry, which has berries that are a pale, ghostly color, sometimes tinged with pink or violet. They tend to be slightly sweeter than their red cousins. The tree is native to

Sweeter than candy, white mulberries ripen in late summer or early autumn. In China, white mulberry root is used to treat coughs. Red and black mulberries were once eaten in America as a folk cure for fevers.

Asia, where the leaves are used both to treat liver ailments and as food for silk-worms. Dried white mulberries are an especially nice cooking ingredient and can be used much like raisins in baking.

Historic though they are, the white and red mulberries do not require the careful pampering that others antiques need to thrive. Ordinary, preferably alkaline, garden soil and a sunny spot in the garden are all these hardy trees require to be content, flourishing in zones 5 to 9.

VEGETABLE PAKORAS WITH MULBERRY DIPPING SAUCE

This wonderful appetizer reinterprets the classic Indian pakora, with pine nuts in the batter and a tangy mulberry sauce for dipping. As the pakoras are somewhat spicy, it's nice to serve them with cold beer.

BATTER:
1/2 cup pine nuts
1 cup chestnut flour (available in Asian groceries) or all-purpose flour
1 teaspoon baking soda
1 teaspoon cream of tartar
1 teaspoon salt
1/2 teaspoon cayenne pepper
1 teaspoon dried rosemary

FILLING:
1 large head of cauliflower or broccoli, broken into florets, cooked briefly in boiling water and cooled immediately in cold water

Olive oil for frying

Mulberry Dipping Sauce (recipe follows)

Pulverize the pine nuts in a blender or food processor. Mix with the flour, baking soda, cream of tartar, salt, and spices. Add 1 cup plus 1 tablespoon water gradually, stirring constantly, to make a thick batter. Let stand, covered, for 1 hour.

Pour olive oil into a large skillet to a depth of 1/2 inch and place over medium-high heat. Stir the batter well, dip the vegetable pieces into the batter, and fry them until golden brown. Drain on paper towels and serve hot with Mulberry Dipping Sauce. **SERVES 6 TO 8**

MULBERRY DIPPING SAUCE

1 1/2 cups fresh mulberries plus 1 tablespoon sugar (or, if out of season, 1 1/2 cups mulberry jam)

2 tablespoons brown mustard
2 tablespoons horseradish

Combine all ingredients and mix well, mashing fresh mulberries thoroughly; whir in food processor to improve consistency, if desired.

OLIVE, *Olea europaea*

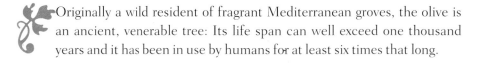Originally a wild resident of fragrant Mediterranean groves, the olive is an ancient, venerable tree: Its life span can well exceed one thousand years and it has been in use by humans for at least six times that long.

The olive is linked with the ancient maritime country of Phoenicia, now known as Lebanon and Syria. In and around that formerly illustrious kingdom, olive oil was used to keep temple lamps glowing and was certainly part of the cuisine.

It was also a profitable cash crop. Phoenician clay vessels filled with olive oil were transported throughout the known world, including Greece, a country that quickly got in on the olive oil trade. The cargo of ill-fated voyages, Phoenician jars and Grecian amphorae have been found littering ocean floors and riverbeds in regions as diverse as Spain, the British Isles, and even the Crimean coast.

Recognizing a good thing when they saw it, the Greeks quickly claimed the olive as their own (just as they adopted the Phoenician idea of the alphabet), and by the time the Phoenician empire was fading out, around the fourth century B.C., Greece had firmly integrated olives into their cooking and trading as well as their culture. The Greeks even went so far as to rewrite history, saying that the olive tree was a gift from the goddess Athena to her beloved namesake city, Athens. A symbol of peace then as now, the olive branch was carried by messengers on peaceful missions.

Ancient Greeks also used olive oil to clean and anoint their bodies, as the Romans did later. Soldiers who spent long periods of time in the wilderness would cover themselves with olive oil to trap body heat. The famous Greek athletes of the early Olympic games rubbed aching muscles with olive oil. This

THE HERBAL GROVE
90

*Orderly
Mediterranean olive
groves are daily
visited by their
grower to check the
progress of the fruit.
Traditionalists
harvest only by hand,
scorning devices that
knock the olives off
the branches to the
ground and damage
the fruit.*

practice is quite alive today, as olive oil infused with a soothing skin herb—such as calendula—is a favorite for massage.

Romans, too, rejoiced in olives, popping them into their mouths with the same frequency that modern-day Americans snack on potato chips. The olive was a versatile food for upper-crust Romans—a popular appetizer and postprandial breath refresher at banquets—while also being without question the staple food of the peasant class.

The olive tree is still essential to Mediterranean and southern European cookery and its flavor seems to be most popular in dishes involving *simple* ingredients. Try eggs scrambled in olive oil, and you'll never make them any other way again. The Spanish consume untold quantities of khaki green and ebony olives as tapas (small bar snacks) and use olive oil to prepare everything from tortillas (omelets) to garlic soups to *torrijas* (delicious fried breads dusted with sugar or cinnamon). Olive oil brings out the flavor of fish, is the perfect complement to garlic mayonnaise, and is an aromatic fillip to simple salads.

Almost everyone is familiar with Italian garlic bread, but people sometimes omit the essential ingredient: a generous dousing of olive oil. And rather than toasting the bread, consider making *bruschetta*. To do so, grill thick slices of peasant bread, rub them with garlic, and then sprinkle on the olive oil. Add a few fresh tomato cubes if you like. You can also quickly use olive oil to make a *tapenade* to spread on bread, mix with mashed potatoes, or drizzle over grilled vegetables or artichokes.

The secret to making the most success of olive cookery is to obtain the finest quality. Avoid both jarred supermarket olives and bargain oils, for they do not come close to conveying true flavor. Seek out specialty purveyors of finer products; the difference in price is negligible compared to the relative quality of the

Olive oil sampling is as serious and complex a business as wine tasting and similar descriptions are used, such as "soft and velvety," "fruity and reminiscent of bitter almonds," or "a delicate bouquet." Here, a Spanish grower samples a luxury item: the first partial extraction of the first pressing.

products. Acquaint yourself with the vast body of Spanish, Grecian, and Italian oils, which vary in color from a pale straw to a misty green and offer tastes ranging from fruity to peppery. And remember that olive oil connoisseurs rate an oil on its fragrance. The oil usually needs to be heated slightly to become fully fragrant. Use virgin (unrefined) oils for salads, vegetables, and other dishes in which its flavor truly makes a difference, and reserve the lesser-quality oils for frying. Store olive oils away from light and heat to retain their potency.

Aside from its culinary and cosmetic properties, the olive is an herbal tree simply because of its nutrient content. Nutritionists have observed that there is a lower rate of heart disease and arteriosclerosis among the native population in the Mediterranean countries than in that of northern Europe and America. It has been hypothesized that their olive-oil–rich diets account for this difference, as well as the smaller amounts of meat and dairy products that they consume.

Olive oil contains no cholesterol and is thought to actually reduce cholesterol in the bloodstream. It is digested more easily than other oils, partly because it contains chlorophyll, which aids absorption, and also because its fragrance actually stimulates gastric juices. Olive oil is also thought to make the liver function more efficiently, stimulate bone growth, and even reduce high blood pressure.

Unless you live in a Mediterraneanlike-climate with full sun, rocky or chalky soil, and little rainfall in zone 9, it would probably be pointless to attempt olive cultivation. This may not seem so bad if you keep in mind that many olive trees don't bear fruit for years after they're planted. The Franciscan missionaries were true Spaniards who couldn't survive without the olive. They introduced this lovely tree to Southern California with great success centuries ago, and some large, old specimens still thrive there. The olive tree is actually an ever-

Centuries-old olive oil vats extracted oils without heating or refining—the same way the best virgin grades are made today. The benefits of olive oil are many: it reduces cholesterol, is more digestible than other oils and fats, and may play a role in the lower incidence of heart disease in the Mediterranean.

THE HERBAL TREES

green, with elliptic leaves and diminutive spring flowers. Wherever they grow, olives are harvested from September through November and sometimes later. The fruits blacken as they age.

Though most of us think we fully appreciate the olive, the closer we inspect its marvelous products, the more we admire this ancient tree.

Two Tree Tapenade

A duet of herbal trees distinguishes this tapenade, made special with the unusual addition of pine nuts.

1 cup imported black olives, pitted
3 cloves garlic, crushed
1 tablespoon capers, or to taste
2 teaspoons pine nuts
4 tablespoons olive oil
1 tablespoon lemon juice

Freshly ground black pepper to taste
1 small loaf peasant-type bread, cut into $1/2$-inch slices
Olive slices for garnish
Chopped parsley for garnish

Place all the ingredients except the bread and garnishes in a blender or food processor and puree. Heat a broiler and toast the slices of bread on one side. Spread the untoasted sides with tapenade and broil for 3 to 5 minutes. Alternatively, serve tapenade cold on toasted bread. Garnish with sliced olives and parsley. **MAKES ABOUT 1 CUP; SERVES 2 TO 4 AS AN APPETIZER**

Marinated Shrimp Carpaccio

Named for carpaccio, the sliced beef dish that requires no cooking, this elegant shrimp concoction can be served as an appetizer or light entrée. It derives its complex yet pleasing taste from herbs and an olive oil vinaigrette.

½ pound shrimp
Salt and freshly ground white pepper to taste
2 tablespoons sherry vinegar
4 tablespoons olive oil
1 teaspoon fresh fines herbes blend (parsley, dill, chervil, and chives), finely chopped
Mixed greens (chicory, endive, lettuce, watercress) or mesclun

Marinated Shrimp Carpaccio calls for the finest olive oil on your shelf. It's recommended that you have two other grades on hand: one for cooking and frying and another for dressing salads and blending into sauces.

Clean the shrimp well, wrap them in plastic, and flatten them to a thickness of ¼ inch or less with a mallet or your fist. Unwrap the shrimp, place them in a shallow glass dish, and season with salt and pepper.

In a bowl, whisk together the vinegar and olive oil. Pour over the shrimp, cover with plastic wrap, and refrigerate for 1 to 2 hours.

Sprinkle the shrimp with fines herbes and serve very cold, accompanied by mixed greens. **SERVES 2**

The restaurant Paradis of Madrid and New York City contributed this recipe.

SOURWOOD, *Oxydendrum arboreum*

Even in winter, when its clusters of small fragrant white flowers are months in the offing and its oblong sour-tasting leaves—chewed as an old trail remedy for thirst—have not yet appeared, sourwood can be recognized year-round by its deeply furrowed bark.

The only member of its genus, *Oxydendrum* (derived from Greek words meaning "sour" and "tree"), the stately sourwood, or sorrel tree, stands alone in many ways.

Its common name alludes to its sour-tasting leaves, which turn scarlet in autumn. Some people feel that the young leaves have a pleasant, lemony taste and advocate chewing on them, while to other palates the taste is acrid. The oblong leaves have been made into a tea used to treat everything from asthma to indigestion. The bark is deeply furrowed, also sour, and has a pleasant texture; it was once chewed by native tribes to ease mouth pains.

In summer, watch for the gorgeous, fragrant white flowers that grow in pendulous sprays. You will probably notice a great many bees around these flowers, for they are the source of sourwood honey, the Rolls-Royce of honeys. A wonderful accompaniment to classic Southern biscuits, a healthful addition to teas, and even a pure beauty aid for the skin, this honey has the aromatic hint of sourwood's blossoms. Southerners warn the potential buyer to be wary of what's sold as sourwood honey: Certain purveyors have been known to dilute the honey with vegetable oils to get the higher price that sourwood honey can command.

There's no question that sourwood merits home cultivation. The tree does well in zones 5 to 9. In the wild, the tree reaches about fifty feet high, yet it will probably not grow this tall on your property. It is rather slow-growing, prefers sun but will grow in shade, and likes an acid soil with a pH of 4 to 5.5. Sourwood is especially abundant in the Southeast, though it also grows in the Midwest and as far north as Pennsylvania.

For those looking to cultivate an apiary, sourwood is an especially nice choice. Plant it near a traditional herbal bee garden of thyme, lemon balm, clover, and borage, and you will have won the hearts of local bumblebees.

*In the American
South, sourwood
honey is legendary
for its exquisite flavor
and folk healing
potential. Old-timers
take it with whiskey
for the common cold
and spread it on their
faces to smooth
the skin.*

Sourwood Cough Treatment

2 tablespoons honey
4 tablespoons lemon juice
1 cup whiskey

Mix well and take as needed, especially at bedtime.

Sourwood Facial Therapy

*Sourwood honey is a fine way to
clean and condition the skin.
Spread it over the face and wait 10
to 15 minutes. Wash with warm
water.*

Sourwood Tonic

*Some folks say a tablespoon of
sourwood honey is a good tonic and
should be taken every day.*

Steven Mazarky of the Green Shutters Restaurant in Clayton, Georgia, offers these suggestions
for using sourwood honey. At the restaurant, the honey is especially exquisite with his homemade
biscuits!

DATE PALM, *Phoenix dactylifera*

*Spreading its
frondlike branches,
the date palm has
earned the
reputation among
Assyrians and
Egyptians as the Tree
of Life—indeed,
these palms can
thrive for centuries.*

In the province of Alicante, Spain, within the charming and unassuming town of Elche, grow four hundred thousand palms, the largest such grove in all of Europe. This species, which thrives on the Mediterranean breezes, is the common date palm, yet the people of the town consider the trees to be anything but common. They treat the grove, and particularly its inner sanctuary, El Huerto del Cura (the Curate's Orchard), with deep respect. There, as everywhere in this Christian country, the palm is one of the most significant religious symbols.

There is a local, quite strange legend in Elche—known throughout Spain as the City of Palms—that the pit of the date is actually *la dente del Virgen,* a part of the Virgin Mary's tooth, that gave life to the palm tree. Elcheans also take credit for originating the custom of using the palm to celebrate Palm Sunday. The story of Jesus' triumphant reception in Jerusalem by the locals with palm fronds has been celebrated throughout Europe since at least the fifth century, using evergreen boughs. Elcheans, however, celebrated the holiday with actual palms and eventually began to trade them throughout Spain. To this day, Elche still holds medieval miracle plays during Lent with date palms as a central motif. Every year, the crowns of many of Elche's palms are gathered in to create straight-lined leaves, which dry to a yellowish white. These branches are used in Palm Sunday services.

The palm came to Spain from Africa. It was brought and planted by Moorish conquerors. The Moors were introduced to the palm by the Phoenicians, the ancient maritime nation of southwest Asia. As with the olive, the Phoenicians shared the wealth of the palm and established groves of them throughout the Mediterranean in their outpost colonies.

Among the Assyrians and Egyptians, palms were represented in art as the Tree of Life, and were thought to increase fertility, probably because of their prolific

fruits. Egyptians believed that dates were one of the few palatable foods for those who had passed on to the afterworld, a curious parallel to certain northern European beliefs about the apple, another Tree of Life fruit thought to be eaten in the great beyond. In John Milton's *Paradise Lost,* the date palm appears in the "woody theatre" of Eden, along with cedar and fir.

The date, which ripens in December, is a wonderful natural energy source. When dried, it contains phosphorus (essential to bones and teeth), niacin (one of the B-complex vitamins, which convert carbohydrates into energy), vitamin B_2 (crucial to biochemical processes), iron (a component of hemoglobin, and thus necessary for healthy red blood cells), and high levels of potassium (an essential nutrient that corrects chemical imbalances). Fresh dates also contain magnesium, an enzyme activator.

Date palms can live for several centuries and thrive in frost-free places. They grow in vast plantations in Africa, India, the American Southwest, and California (zones 9 through 11). They were originally brought to California by Spanish conquistadores settling their new colonies. These spectacular trees are also grown as ornamentals in parts of northern Europe, but will not bear fruit there because of the cooler climate. Fruiting date palms enjoy a rather polygamous existence, as one male is planted to pollinate every seventy or so females. If you live in a suitable climate for growing date palms, plant container-grown specimens in a sunny spot with a well-drained soil. They will grow quickly, possibly reaching sixty feet, and require constant watering, although they are damaged by rain, which is why American growers often shield their trees with paraffin-coated paper cloaks.

Eating dates will probably not make you immortal, but these ancient fruits will certainly keep you healthy.

DATE-ALMOND TAPAS

As guests bite into this impressive appetizer, they will be delighted by the unexpected crunch of almond, hidden away beneath each bacon-wrapped date.

16 pitted dates
16 almonds
8 slices bacon, cut in half crosswise

Preheat oven to 500 degrees. Put one almond inside each date, wrap the dates in bacon, and secure with a toothpick. Bake for 15 to 20 minutes, until bacon is crisp, and serve as an appetizer. **SERVES 8**

This recipe was inspired by El Capitan Restaurant at the Jardineria Huerto del Cura in Elche, Spain.

Aside from their delicious taste, bite-sized Date Almond Tapas offer vitamin B6, copper, magnesium, and iron.

WHITE PINE, *Pinus strobus*   PINYON PINE, *Pinus edulis*
ITALIAN STONE PINE, *Pinus pinea*

Rituals, whether they be those of native tribes of the American Southwest or of European cultures, often serve a purpose that supersedes superstition. The pine provides a perfect illustration of this point. Among the Cherokee, it is a common practice for families to create a fire of pine boughs in the home and walk around it many times in a circle; if there is an infant in the family, they will pass the baby through the smoke. Mysterious and enigmatic as it may seem, the ritual serves a very practical purpose: It is for purification, for oil of pine is an antiseptic and a disinfectant, and the oils are released in smoke when the branches are lit.

Indeed, the luscious smoke of burning pine wafts back over many centuries. The perpetual fire at Delphi, Greece, was fueled by pine. In the second century B.C., pre-Christian Italians created tremendous pinewood fires in honor of now-obscure deities; noblemen inspired by the deities or perhaps by the monetary rewards for their bravery would walk over the scathing coals in a purification ritual. In plague-ridden medieval Europe, pine branches hung over the bed were thought to keep evil spirits and sickness from entering the home. It is logical to assume that such practices arose on account of the pine's reputation as a purifier.

Such beliefs persist today, in various forms. Some people still have faith in the magical qualities of the pine, burning the needles in the hearth and strewing them about their floors to purify their homes. Even the most unsuperstitious among us use commercial pine-oil preparations to clean. And, regardless of magical inclinations, who wouldn't enjoy the invigorating scent of pine needles in potpourri or pine oil in the bath?

There are more than one hundred species of pine, but it is the North American white pine that has inspired the most usages. Native Americans used to dine on the bark, but as Euell Gibbons reported in *Stalking the Healthful Herbs,* its

bark is bad, and its bite is worse—white pine bark is not a particularly delicious substance. Although it does contain vitamin C, and the dried inner bark was once a major ingredient in cough syrups, the taste is very bitter. Perhaps the most pleasant contemporary use for it is making tea from its needles. For example, characters in Tim Robbins's *Another Roadside Attraction*, published in 1971, enjoy a communal forest breakfast of toasted puffball mushrooms, yogurt, and fresh pine needle tea. The vitamin A– and C–rich tea is made by steeping fresh pine needles in water. Young, spring-harvested needles make the nicest, most aromatic tea.

Pine resin, the sticky substance found in the wood of pines, naturally wards off insect pests. Like the resins of frankincense, myrrh, and balm of Gilead, pine resin also has antibacterial qualities. Southwestern Native American tribes used pine resin to purify and seal wounds. In Colonial times the Europeans who came to America used it to produce various products. Turpentine, the original linoleum (before it was synthesized), and amber (often used to make jewelry) are all by-products of pine resin.

This classic forest tree can live for hundreds of years, reaching heights of 150 feet under ideal conditions. It grows in zones 3 to 7 and thrives in moist soils, as long as they are well drained. The tree does particularly well transplanted in a ball of earth, as opposed to container planting. Unfortunately, white pine blister rust, a fungal disease that can kill entire trees and some neighboring plants, is still a problem in some parts of the United States. So, check with your local county extension service to ensure that it is safe to grow white pine in your area.

The pine family has a remarkable range of offerings. In America, while the white pine of the Northeast was feeding the Iroquois and Mohegans with its bark, the pinyon pine, generally found in the mountains of Arizona and New

The white pine inspired the white men's name for Indians (adirondack, or "tree eater") because they dined on its dried edible bark. This tree can also be used to make a twig tea, and its soft, fragrant needles are ideal for potpourri.

Mexico (zones 6 to 7), was providing an abundant edible bounty for the Navajo and Pueblo tribes. It is not a large tree, only in rare cases reaching beyond twenty-five-feet high. Its cones contain delicious seeds, known as pinyon (or pine) nuts, which can be enjoyed raw or roasted.

The European counterpart of this tree, the Italian stone pine, also grows in warm areas (zones 9 to 10). Like its New World relative, it yields delicious seeds, which in Spain and Italy are prodigiously used in candies, sauces, and especially as an accompaniment to fish. In Spain the seeds are called *piñones;* in Italy, *pinoles.* Some of the most remarkable cookies one could ever hope to taste are handcrafted by nuns in the south of Spain using a secret-ingredient flour mixed with local pine nuts. Oddly, pine nuts were far more commonly used in British cookery in medieval times, when they were mixed with dried fruits, such as currants, raisins, and dates, and used in meat and fish dishes.

Large groves of this tree dot southern Europe, Italy and Spain in particular, and can also be found in parts of northern Africa. It has a graceful, unmistakable parasol shape, which also makes it a lovely shade tree. This tree can grow considerably higher than its North American cousin, to eighty feet, and survives droughts with ease.

Laced with dawn mists, the wild European pinyon pine (Pinus pinea) *inspires imaginative flights of fancy. This marvelous tree provides the familiar pine nut that's an essential ingredient of pesto.*

Swiss
MOUNTAIN TEA

This tea features ingredients from two classic herbal trees: the pine and the linden, the latter tree much enjoyed in Europe but little known in the United States. All the herbs in the recipe are usually available at your herbalist, and if there's something you can't find, the tea won't suffer from a few missing ingredients. Many people associate herbal teas with winter colds, but this healthy beverage tastes great and can be enjoyed year-round. It makes a nice breakfast drink, a pleasant four o'clock tea, and a great iced tea that will stay fresh, covered, in the refrigerator for a little more than a week.

3.2 grams (.11 ounce) linden flowers (*Tilia europaea* or *Tilia americana*)

2.8 grams (.10 ounce) European cowslip (*Primula officinalis*)

2 grams (.07 ounce) woodruff (*Asperula odorata*)

2 grams (.07 ounce) lemon balm (*Melissa officinalis*)

2 grams (.07 ounce) calendula (*Calendula officinalis*)

2 grams (.07 ounce) red clover (*Trifolium pratense*)

2 grams (.07 ounces) white pine buds (*Pinus strobus*)

1.2 grams (.04 ounce) mint (*Mentha spicata*)

1.2 grams (.04 ounces) bee balm (*Monarda didyma*)

To Make Traditional Tea:

Brew the tea by using 1 teaspoon of herbs per cup of cold water. Add herbs to water in pot and bring to a boil, stirring occasionally. Remove from heat, cover, and steep for 15 minutes.

Strain and sweeten with honey or brown sugar.

To Make Iced Tea:

Place 6 heaping tablespoons of herbs into 6 quarts of cold water. Bring to a boil, stirring occasionally. Remove from heat, cover, and let steep overnight. The next morning, strain the tea and add 1 large can frozen lemonade. **Makes about 6 quarts**

Herbalist Dora Gerber, of New York State's Swissette Herb Farm, inherited this recipe from her Swiss grandmother, and so she likes to think of it as "Mama Gerber's Herbal Tea." As long as her parents were alive, they, too, used to harvest the ingredients in the mountains of Switzerland.

PINE NUT DUMPLINGS

With a pesto filling mingled with brown rice, this dish is a healthy alternative to fried take-out–style dumplings. It makes a delicious appetizer, but also serves beautifully as an entree.

PESTO:
4 tablespoons pine nuts, toasted
1/2 cup extra-virgin olive oil
3 garlic cloves, chopped into small pieces
1 cup fresh basil leaves

3 tablespoons grated Pecorino, Parmesan, or Romano cheese
Squeeze of lemon

1 cup cooked brown rice
8 steamed cabbage leaves

Preheat oven to 325 degrees. Toast pine nuts for 8 to 10 minutes, turning once, and remove when lightly tan. Do not let them get too dark.

In a blender or food processor, puree oil, garlic, and 2 tablespoons toasted nuts. Add basil a little at a time. Add cheese and lemon and continue to puree until smooth. Transfer mixture to a bowl and blend in additional 2 tablespoons of whole toasted nuts with rice.

In a steamer or double boiler, steam separated cabbage leaves for approximately 3 minutes, or until slightly translucent and pliable.

Divide pesto-rice mixture equally among the cabbage leaves. Roll leaves closed and tuck ends under. **SERVES 8 AS AN APPETIZER, 4 AS AN ENTREE**

As the Long Hungry River of Tennessee meanders in the background, a balm of Gilead tree flourishes on its banks, lovingly taking up water with its roots.

BALM OF GILEAD, *Populus balsamifera*

Perhaps it is the soothing, balsamic scent and lovely appearance of balm of Gilead that has made this tree the source of a favorite folk remedy for centuries. Or maybe the tree's salicin content, related to aspirin for its ability to relieve pain, is responsible for its remedial reputation. In the West, *Populus balsamifera* subspecies *trichocarpa,* the black cottonwood, is used in the same medicinal capacity. Balm of Gilead shares its name with another plant, *Commiphora meccanensis,* which is mentioned in the Bible. The biblical region of Gilead, now known as Jordan, was renowned for this plant and its balm. New World settlers named *Populus balsamifera* balm of Gilead in reference to the biblical plant, which symbolizes healing in the Scriptures.

If you embark on a balm of Gilead pilgrimage, perhaps you ought to buy a boat, for, like its far-flung cousin the willow, this tree thrives near water. It is often found growing along riversides and creeks in eastern North America from Canada southward. Keep in mind that the tree may grow as high as one hundred feet, but is usually far smaller. The older the tree, the darker and more gnarled the bark. Its early spring "flowers" are actually catkins. As summer comes on, pretty oval leaves festoon the tree.

Once you have identified balm of Gilead by its warm-weather finery, mark the spot and return in winter. This is the prime time to harvest the sticky, resinous, plump buds of balm of Gilead: Their intense aroma alone will make the journey worthwhile.

As late as the 1920s and 1930s, people would make similar journeys to collect "gilly buds" so that they could sell them to drug companies for use in their various pain-relieving concoctions. The buds were also valued for home use. Winter-harvested buds were added to rum and strained out after several weeks, then the scented liquid could be used on cuts and wounds. The buds were also renowned as cures for chest complaints. Do-it-yourself doctors

Balm of Gilead buds were once an important ingredient in cough syrups and avidly collected by backwoods entrepreneurs eager to sell "gilly buds" to pharmaceutical companies. Today, do-it-yourselfers make the buds into a salve.

would make a tincture of the buds by adding them to vodka for two weeks or so and then straining out the liquid and taking it in teaspoon doses, much like cough medicine.

If nothing ails you, you can still enjoy the fragrance of balm of Gilead. Try adding it to potpourri or sachets so that you needn't go on a long trek to enjoy the buds year-round. Remember, too, that these are fast-growing trees—which is why they are such favorites for reforestation. They thrive in zones 2 to 6, and even farther south. If you provide a moist soil and obtain stock from a reliable nursery, you may be enjoying a miniature herbal grove in a matter of months.

GROVE POTPOURRI

One of the nicest qualities of trees is that many have fragrant leaves and buds even in the middle of winter, before flowers have come into bloom. This is a wonderful way to bring a woodland scent indoors and cheer the home while it is still cold outdoors. Because essential oils can sometimes create skin reactions, use of gloves is recommended when preparing this. Based on scent, increase amounts of essential oils used to your liking.

20 winter-harvested balm of Gilead buds
1 cup pine needles
15 to 20 small pine cones*
1 cup dried rosemary
1 cup dried violet petals
¹/₄ cup ground orrisroot
5 drops oil of pine
5 drops ylang-ylang oil

In a glass bowl or plastic container, mix together dry ingredients. Add oils drop by drop and stir with a wooden spoon. Transfer to a glass or plastic container with a close-fitting lid, and place in a cool, dark place for at least 3 weeks to cure. Stir from time to time. After the necessary amount of time has passed, display in a decorative bowl or several bowls, adding whole dried blossoms of any flower to the top for a decorative effect.

*Pine cones are nice to display on their own. To give them scent, cure them in glass or plastic containers for 2 weeks or more with a few drops of your favorite essential oils.

BALM OF GILEAD SALVE

This marvelous and sweetly fragrant salve is made from buds harvested from fall until early spring, before leaf opening. Early spring is preferable, since that is when buds are at their most resinous, but some people like to harvest them when they're a bit frozen and easier to handle. The salve is great for dry and chapped skin, and even for athlete's foot. It can also be mixed with other herbal oils, such as lavender and calendula.

Balm of Gilead buds (amount adjusts to size of jar)
Olive oil to cover

Beeswax (1 ounce per cup of olive oil)

Harvest balm of Gilead buds to fill a jar partially, leaving some room at top. Add olive oil so that it covers the buds by ¼ to ½ inch. Seal the jar with a lid and shake well.

Leave in a moderately warm place (such as a kitchen, a bathroom, or near a radiator or wood stove) for a minimum of 2 weeks, but preferably a month or longer. Shake jar at least once a day, sometimes turning it upside down.

Strain out oil into a pan. Grate 1 ounce of beeswax for every cup of oil and add to the oil. Heat very gently, until the beeswax melts. Test the consistency by dipping a teaspoon into the mixture, removing it, and putting it in the refrigerator for a minute. Remove and test the salve. It should have a nice, smooth consistency. If it's too hard, add a little more oil; if it's too soft, add a bit more beeswax.

Stir the mixture and pour it into jars. Seal and allow to harden before using.

Herbalist Carol McGrath of Victoria, British Columbia, Canada, contributed this recipe, which she uses with the western North American balm of Gilead, *Populus balsamifera* subspecies *trichocarpa.*

ALMOND, *Prunus dulcis*

Standing on a dusty country road in Spain, you can inspect the beautiful trees growing in the orchard spreading off to the sides. They certainly resemble peach trees, but there is something different about them. So you ask a passing goatherder, his flock pausing from time to time to lean back on their haunches and sample that which grows in the branches, if he knows the identity of this species. *"El almendro, claro,"* he says, and opens a nut to reveal a smooth, creamy almond.

Upon first inspection, many people mistake the almond tree for the peach, for the almond's fuzzy green stone greatly resembles that of its close cousin. The two are, in fact, both members of the rose family and even share the same genus. Like the peach, the almond is an important herbal tree, but it is more sensitive, both in its fragile growth habits (the tree does not take well to frost) and in the lore that surrounds it (which is tightly linked with romance).

The ancient Greeks wove a charming myth around the almond tree: A young woman engaged to an errant sailor pines after her fiancé and becomes so forlorn that she dies. The gods take pity on her and let her live on eternally as the almond tree. She had a better fate than many other mythological women, who were variously turned into mint, to be trampled on, and into myrrh, to eternally cry resin tears. The pretty pink spring blossoms of almond poetically represent the young woman's undying love.

Almonds needn't languish in a kitchen canister. Cooks everywhere should take inspiration from the imaginative uses of the nut in Mediterranean countries. Almonds are a staple of the national cuisine of Spain and are used in fragrant soups (said to be an aphrodisiac), toasted as *tapas*, baked in *Roscon de Reyes* (Kings' Day Cake), served on January 6 in commemoration of the journey of the Magi to Bethlehem, and made into cookies and marzipan. Greeks use almonds generously in desserts, while Moroccans use them in main courses,

The almond is a small, graceful tree that much resembles the peach. Curiously, we eat peach flesh and discard the stone, while with the almond we crack open the pit to gain access to the nut within. Not just for eating, almonds are wonderful to grind up and use as buffing cleansers on the face.

such as chicken. And in France, such dishes as trout almandine attest to this nut's versatility as a main-course ingredient. Almonds contain B vitamins, calcium, iron, and phosphorous—which prevents mental fatigue, spurs bone growth, and keep teeth healthy.

These wonderful nuts also have a long history as an ingredient in cosmetics. Amandine was a perfumed cleanser popular in Victorian times. It was made from attar of rose and almond oil. The French created *Pate d'amande au Miel,* a cleansing mixture of honey, eggs, almond oil, and blanched and ground almonds mixed with perfumes. And years before packaged face masks were popular, women refined their skin with a mask of almond paste, often scented with rose- or orange-flower water. Smoothed directly on the skin, almond oil makes a rich moisturizer and massage oil and can also be used as a hair moisturizer. If you want to try this, use the oil in *small* amounts to keep your hair from getting too oily.

Grown in groves throughout the Mediterranean as well as in California and other western states with mild winters, the almond is a small tree (reaching about thirty feet) that doesn't tolerate late-spring frosts or too much wind. If you live in an area conducive to growing this versatile tree, be sure that its fragile blossoms are protected from harsh weather surprises. Though it does best in zones 8 to 10, there *are* cold-hardy almond varieties, and, as John Gerard reported in his late-sixteenth-century *Herball,* "The naturall place of the Almond is in the hot regions, yet we have them in our London gardens and orchards in great plenty." If you live in a region where late-spring frosts occur, plant only varieties that flower late in the season so that their blossoms stand a less likely chance of being damaged and can set fruit. Bear in mind also that, unless they are specifically labeled as such, almonds are *not* self-fertile. For successful pollination, you will need another simultaneously blooming almond tree planted nearby, or, if space is tight, in the same planting hole.

The almond is not especially particular about soil, though it must be well drained. From the time of planting, an almond tree will grow for about four years before bearing fruit. In the dormant season, keep the tree pruned in an open-cup shape so that all branches receive light. As with the apple tree, save the pruned branches, dry them in a garage, and use them cut up into chunks for grilling to impart a nutty flavor to foods. Just before grilling, soak them in water for a half hour. Even if growing an almond tree is out of the question, northerners needn't despair, for the gifts of the almond are always available, no matter what the weather.

ALMANDINE FACIAL MASK

Almonds are the foundation of this facial mask, which features fresh mint for its stimulating qualities and marshmallow for its softening effects. All herbs are easily grown and readily available at the herbalist. It is most effective to combine the ingredients in a blender or food processor. Begin with 1/2 cup whole almonds (which will chop down to about 4 generous tablespoons), chopping them into a meal with a bit of texture to it so that the almonds can act as an exfoliant. You will have to turn the blender on and off several times and scrape down the mixture so that it fully combines.

4 tablespoons ground almonds
10 sprigs fresh mint
2 tablespoons plain yogurt

1 scant tablespoon dried marshmallow root

Grind almonds until powdery but still textured. Add mint and yogurt and blend. Add marshmallow and continue blending until paste is formed. **MAKES 2 MASKS**

AJO BLANCO (ALMOND-GARLIC GAZPACHO)

The summertime counterpart to hot Almond-Garlic Soup, Ajo Blanco—a cold almond soup literally translated as "white garlic"—is a classic summertime dish from the hot region of Andalusia, and is served throughout Spain.

¹/₂ **cup olive oil**
12 cloves garlic (or more to taste)
1 cup ice water
¹/₂ **pound slivered or sliced**
    blanched almonds
4 slices stale white bread, crusts
    removed
Sherry vinegar
3 cups vegetable stock
1 teaspoon salt
Freshly ground white pepper to
    taste
12 red grapes, peeled, for garnish

Served cold in summer, Ajo Blanco is a kind of gazpacho. It has a rather high protein content, as well as impressive amounts of calcium, iron, and vitamin E.

Put the olive oil in a saucepan over very low heat and sauté the garlic until wilted (but not browned). Add the ice water, raise the heat to medium-low, and simmer for 25 to 30 minutes. Set aside to cool.

When the garlic mixture has cooled, combine it with the almonds and puree in a blender or food processor. Soak the bread in sherry vinegar. Add the bread, stock, salt, and pepper to the blender or processor and puree again.

Chill, covered, for at least 2 hours to allow the flavors to blend. Serve cold, garnished with 3 grapes in each bowl. **SERVES 4**

ALMOND-GARLIC SOUP

With your mortar and pestle in hand, preparing this soup feels as if you're blending some ancient herbal elixir. Indeed, this healthful soup is like a tonic on a winter's day.

1 pound sliced or slivered
   blanched almonds
3 hard-boiled egg yolks
1 pint vegetable stock
1 pint light cream
2 cloves garlic, minced
Salt and freshly ground pepper to
   taste
Yerba buena, mint, or apple slices
   for garnish

Pound the almonds and egg yolks together with a mortar and pestle to make a paste.

Put the almond paste in a saucepan over low heat and very gradually add the vegetable stock, stirring constantly to keep the soup smooth. Add the cream, garlic, and salt and pepper and stir well. Continue stirring until the mixture is very hot (but not boiling), 10 to 15 minutes. Pour into serving bowls and top with the garnish of your choice. **SERVES 6**

This recipe was inspired by a soup served at Colombia Tipico Restaurante in Granada, Spain.

*Almond-Garlic Soup
   is brimming with
   health-boosting
   ingredients.*

XATO SAUCE

This spicy almond sauce is very popular in the Catalonian region of Spain. It can be served with grilled chicken or fish and is sometimes brushed on during cooking.

4 tomatoes
2 to 3 cloves garlic, peeled
1 or more fresh hot chili peppers, seeds removed
$^1\!/_2$ cup slivered or sliced blanched almonds

Salt and freshly ground black pepper to taste
$^1\!/_2$ cup olive oil
$^1\!/_4$ cup wine vinegar

Preheat oven to 350 degrees. Place the whole tomatoes and garlic in an oiled baking pan and roast for about 20 minutes. Remove from the oven and set aside to cool.

Place the chili peppers and nuts on a cookie sheet and toast in the oven for about 8 minutes, turning them over after 4 minutes and being careful not to burn them. Remove from the oven and let cool slightly.

When the tomatoes are cool enough to handle, remove their skins and cores. Place the tomatoes, garlic, chili peppers, nuts, and salt and pepper in a blender or food processor and puree. Slowly add the oil and vinegar while continuing to process. For best results, let the sauce stand, covered, for 4 hours to let the flavor intensify. (It can be used immediately if desired.) **MAKES 3 CUPS**

This sauce is based on a recipe from Alambique Cooking School in Madrid, as are the cookies that follow.

Almond Cookies

Almond cookies are a very Old World–type treat, the kind of fare sold at convent bakeries in small European towns. Here is a no-skimp recipe for making them. Tucked into tins and wrapped with a bow, these make memorable holiday gifts.

1 cup sliced or slivered blanched almonds
1 tablespoon olive oil
3 egg whites
²/₃ cup sugar
1 tablespoon lemon juice
24 whole almonds or ¹/₄ cup pine nuts for garnish

Crisp as biscuits, Almond Cookies are an Old World dessert from the days when simple confections of candied nuts and fruits followed dinner.

Preheat the oven to 300 degrees.

Mix the almonds with the olive oil and spread them on a cookie sheet or in a shallow roasting pan. Toast in the oven, turning occasionally, until light brown, about 10 minutes. Be sure to watch them carefully—the browning proceeds very quickly once it begins. Remove the nuts from the oven and set aside until cool enough to handle. Grind the toasted almonds in a spice grinder or food processor or chop them extremely finely with a knife. Be sure not to overprocess the almonds if using a machine; pulse the grinder or processor on and off very quickly, just until the nuts are fine. (Overprocessing will result in almond butter!) Set aside.

Beat the egg whites to soft peaks in a medium-sized bowl. Gradually add the sugar and lemon juice while continuing to beat. Gently fold in the ground almonds.

Cover a flat cookie sheet with parchment. For each cookie, pour 2 heaping tablespoons of batter, one on top of the other, onto the parchment, and top with a whole almond or a sprinkle of pine nuts. The cookies should be about 3 inches in diameter. Bake for 15 to 20 minutes, or until golden. Slide the parchment with the cookies onto a wire rack and cool completely. Peel the paper off the cookies and serve immediately, or store up to 2 days in an airtight tin with wax paper between the layers. **MAKES 2 DOZEN COOKIES**

ALMOND TART

A delightful cross between a Greek baklava pastry and an old-fashioned American nut pie, this tart crunches with almonds both inside and out.

HONEY SYRUP:
1/2 **cup honey**
3/4 **cup water**
1/2 **lemon**

PASTRY:
1 1/2 **cups all-purpose flour**
1/4 **teaspoon salt**
6 **tablespoons unsalted butter**
2 **tablespoons plus 1 teaspoon
   cold solid vegetable shortening**
3 **to 4 tablespoons cold water**

FILLING:
1 1/2 **cups coarsely chopped mixed
   almonds, pistachios, and
   walnuts**
2 **tablespoons sugar**
1 1/2 **teaspoons cinnamon**
Pinch of ground cloves

TOPPING:
1 **cup whole almonds, blanched**

*With a baklava-like
filling, Almond Tart is
beautifully presented
on the table with a
pleasing swirl of nuts.*

Combine syrup ingredients and simmer until thick enough to coat back of spoon, about 8 minutes. Remove lemon and simmer 3 minutes longer. Cool and refrigerate.

Combine flour and salt in a large bowl. Cut in butter and shortening to the texture of coarse crumbs. Add water 1 tablespoon at a time. Mix gently to form a soft dough. Do not overwork. Chill for 1 hour.

While pastry dough chills, combine and mix filling ingredients and set aside.

Blanch almonds by boiling for 2 minutes. Drain, plunge into cold water, remove hulls.

Preheat oven to 425 degrees. Roll out pastry and line a shallow 10-inch pie pan. Add filling, pat down, arrange blanched almonds on top. Pour over honey syrup. Bake for 10 minutes, reduce heat, and continue to bake at 325 degrees for 30 minutes. **SERVES 8 TO 10**

PEACH, *Prunus persica*

Most of us scarcely give a moment's thought to the peach, but to the Roman Pliny it was the Persian apple. To the Chinese, it was the Tao, or Way. To medieval Europeans, the peach was a succulent gift from China and the irresistible cargo of the Crusades, a magical, curvaceous aphrodisiac. With its delectable flavor, refreshing scent, and coral-colored velvety skin, the peach often calls for a second glance.

Chinese herbalists and laymen alike have long believed that the peach can actually grant immortality simply by being consumed. Grown on Chinese soil for three millennia, the peach is the Occidental equivalent of the Western Tree of Life, traditionally associated with the apple. In fact, along with such other herbal trees as the magnolia and the plum, it was buried in Chinese tombs as an assurance of good "health" in the afterlife.

But the peach is also very much a part of this life. Should a Chinese person hand you a peach, your friendship is sealed. If you visit your new friend's home and see peach branches hanging on the wall or gathered in a vase, rest assured that evil spirits will not interrupt your conversation, as they are said to deter the dark forces. For added protection, string a peach pit around your neck—this is similar to the well-known European belief that garlic thwarts the efforts of vampires. Peach-pit kernels have also been used in Chinese medicine for circulation, although they are toxic in the hands of a novice, as they contain the chemical amygdalin (also found in bitter almonds and apricots). Amygdalin decomposes into prussic acid, a lethal poison with no antidote. In the West, amygdalin is commercially known as laetrile and has been used to treat cancer. However, the National Cancer Institute reports that laetrile is not an effective treatment.

Peach pits make intriguing textural ornaments for gift wrapping when combined with a raffia bow and field-gathered grasses, cones, and dried flowers. This design is by Jas. Kirkland.

The Chinese also once thought that peach branches, in the form of Y- or V-shaped divining rods, would assist people in locating water. (This belief, known in the West as rhabdomancy, has long been practiced with a variety of trees, including hazel, apple, and rowan.)

The peach was brought to Europe in the Middle Ages and quickly gained approval. By Culpeper's time, peach trees were an accepted element in herbalism. "They are nursed in gardens and orchards throughout this land," Culpeper declared in his *Herbal*. He recommended using a peach syrup or conserve as a cure for cholera or jaundice. Certainly the peach's iron and vitamin C content would seem to fortify the human immune system. Nowadays, we eat peach preserves, peach butter, and fresh fruit purely for delight, the healthful benefits notwithstanding. Some Appalachian Mountain people swear by homemade peach brandy as a remedy for anything that ails you. Others warn that too much of this elixir could send you to an early grave. It seems that moderation is the key.

Of course, don't forget about the culinary delights of peaches. Blend them with yogurt for a delicious shake, add them to sherry in a goblet, bake them into pies and cobblers, cook them lightly and then smother them with sour cream or chocolate, stew them into fruit compotes, or serve them with pork or duck.

Beyond the fruit, the narrow, shiny leaves of peaches have their own repertoire of uses. An old French folk tale tells of a man who was bewitched and fell quite ill. The spell could be reversed only by a wizard placing three peach leaves under the sick man's pillow. Culpeper recommended quite a different use: "The leaves of peaches bruised and laid on the belly, kill worms," he contended. Today, the leaves are more reliably employed in facial steams to enliven the complexion. Just be sure the leaves weren't sprayed with pesticides—obtain them from your home orchard, from an organic farmer, or from an herbalist with organic sources.

Most Americans identify the peach strongly with the South, particularly Georgia. The peach certainly thrives in warm climates and enjoys plenty of sun, but there are varieties that can well tolerate winter cold (growing in zones 4 to 8). The peach tends to remain a somewhat small and manageable tree and doesn't thrive much beyond its twentieth birthday. But it takes well to a wide range of soils, sandy loam being a favorite—so long as they are well drained. Peach trees bear fruit only on one-year-old shoots, and once that wood has borne fruit, it never will again. Therefore, it's important to prune during the dormant season to create a cup shape to allow for light to pass through easily to all the branches.

As with its cousin the almond tree, save the pruned branches, dry them in a garage, and cut them into chunks to smoke among barbecue coals. Just before grilling, soak the wood in water for a half hour so that it will smoulder. Foods grilled over peach wood have a slightly sweet taste.

Though most people plant nursery-grown peach trees, it's also possible to grow them from seed. If you try it, use a number of pits to increase your chance of success. Keep in mind that peaches ripen from July to October in the North and from June to July in the South. Obtain ripe fruit, extract the stone, and clean off all the pulp and juice. Plant in autumn, sometime before mid-October, in two-inch-deep soil (following instructions in Chapter 2) or stratify for three months (again following instructions in Chapter 2) prior to planting in spring after the danger of frost has passed. The stratification process will crack the endocarp (outer shell). It sounds slightly complicated, but it's really a fairly simple procedure—and imagine the fun of showing friends a tree you grew from a pit!

If you are still undecided about the merits of the peach, consider the lacy pink springtime blossoms and how they will adorn your garden. All things considered, the peach is not so very demanding, and, magical fruit that it is, can yield much in return for the simple act of planting.

Though associated with the South,
peach trees yield plenty of fruit in northern
climes, such as in this New York State
front yard. The tree is also a beautiful
sight in springtime.

PEACH BUTTER

Peach butter is wonderful with biscuits, toast, and muffins. If you have some fresh raspberries on hand as well, you can turn pound cake or vanilla ice cream into a quick but special dessert. You don't need to make the amount given here: Just remember to use half as much sugar as you do peaches.

8 cups peeled and coarsely
    chopped peaches
4 cups sugar

Squeeze of lemon juice
Cinnamon to taste

Combine the peaches with the sugar, lemon, and cinnamon in a large stainless steel or enamel pot. Bring the mixture to a boil, stirring constantly. Lower the heat and cook slowly for 1 hour, stirring occasionally, until the mixture is thick and smooth.

    Pour into sterilized 8-ounce glass jars and seal immediately with sterilized 2-piece lids. **MAKES ABOUT 4 PINTS**

North Carolina herbalist and folklorist Barbara Duncan, Ph.D., contributed this classic Southern recipe.

PEACH LEAF STEAM

After using this mask, your face will feel both clean and soothed. The peach leaves and peppermint will enliven the complexion, while marshmallow and chamomile soothe. Look for these ingredients at the herbalist.

2 tablespoons dried peach leaves
1 tablespoon dried peppermint

1 tablespoon dried marshmallow
    root
1 tablespoon dried chamomile

Add herbs to a large, broad bowl and cover with about 5 cups boiling water to fill the bowl. Spread a towel over your head and covering the bowl as well so that no steam escapes. Sit for at least 10 minutes or as long as 20 minutes. When finished, follow with rosewater toner or a facial mask (see page 115). **1 STEAM**

LYNCHBURG PEACH PIE

Fresh peach pie is one of life's greatest pleasures. This recipe, spiced with cinnamon and nutmeg, is particularly delicious accompanied by homemade vanilla custard, ice cream, or whipped cream.

Pie Pastry (recipe follows)
¼ cup butter
4 cups peeled, sliced peaches
½ cup firmly packed light brown sugar
1½ teaspoons cinnamon
¼ teaspoon grated nutmeg
1¼ cups heavy cream
½ cup Jack Daniel's whiskey or other good bourbon
2 tablespoons sugar

Served on a bed of blossoms, fresh peach pie is a time-honored use for the usual abundance a single healthy tree can produce.

Make pie pastry and chill.

Preheat oven to 350 degrees. Melt the butter in a heavy saucepan and add the peaches, brown sugar, spices, and cream. Bring to a boil and simmer for 5 minutes, stirring carefully to avoid crushing the peaches. Add the bourbon and continue to cook for 15 minutes or until the mixture is thickened. Remove from heat.

Divide the chilled pastry in half, roll out 2 crusts, and line a 9-inch pie tin with half the pastry. Pour in the peach filling and cover with the remaining pastry. Crimp the edges well to avoid leakage, and prick the top with a fork to allow steam to escape. Sprinkle with 2 tablespoons sugar.

Bake for 40 to 45 minutes, or until light brown. (If the edge of the crust is browning too quickly, place a protective rim of foil over it.) Cool completely on a wire rack before serving. **SERVES 8**

PIE PASTRY (FOR A 2-CRUST PIE)

2 cups flour
1 teaspoon salt
⅛ teaspoon sugar

⅔ cup lard, shortening, or cold
   butter or margarine, or a
   combination
3 to 5 tablespoons ice water

Stir the flour, salt, and sugar together in a bowl. With a pastry blender, 2 knives, or your hands, cut in the lard, shortening, butter, or margarine until the fat is very fine and the mixture looks like coarse cornmeal. (This can also be done in a food processor; transfer to a mixing bowl when complete.)

Add the ice water 1 tablespoon at a time and blend it in with a fork. Use just enough water for the dough to barely hold together in a ball.

Wrap the dough in plastic wrap and chill for 1 hour.

Credit for this recipe goes to Miss Mary Bobo's Boarding House in Lynchburg, Tennessee, courtesy of proprietor Lynne Tolley. See also the Lemon Icebox Pie recipe from Miss Mary Bobo's on page 55.

WILD BLACK CHERRY OR RUM CHERRY, *Prunus serotina*

For as long as mountain people can remember, the wild black cherry has been thought of as a "medicine tree." It grows prolifically along roadsides and in forest clearings throughout North America. This tree can be easily identified by its distinctive white flowers, hanging luxuriously in elongated "grape bunches," creating the perfect setting under which to have a champagne picnic to celebrate the arrival of spring.

But, herbally speaking, the flowers are not the main attraction of the tree. Another common name, lung balm bark, gives a good clue to its other uses. The inner bark of the tree, collected in springtime, is an old-time ingredient for cough syrup. The inner bark has also been made into a tea for stomach upset and for use as a blood tonic. While the bark does indeed exhibit expectorant, astringent, and even digestive qualities, it also produces a sedative effect, for it has been found to contain cyanidelike toxins, especially present in autumn. The wilted leaves are poisonous. Unless you are a trained herbalist, it is better to enjoy this tree for its beauty and its fruits. For an energy-filled tonic, juice freshly picked cherries and drink a glass a day for a week. The fruits contain iron, which imparts vitality, and phosphorous, which provides nourishment for the brain and bones.

Black cherry fruits, which ripen in late summer and early autumn, are quite tiny, and are not as sweet as cultivated cherries (*P. avium*). Just about any dish made with traditional cherries can be made with black cherries (always remove the pits before using). Use them in fruit compotes and pies. You can mix them with the fruit of cultivated cherries to increase the sweetness and the bulk. You might also try making traditional Hungarian cherry soup with a half-and-half mixture of wild black cherries and sweet cherries.

Cherries and alcohol are a classic combination; in fact, another common name of wild black cherry is rum cherry. Europeans use sweet cherries to create a

Pendulant wild black cherry flowers bedizen the tree in springtime.

*Resembling garnet
beads, wild black
cherries ripen at
summer's end; too
sour to eat fresh or
cook with, they are
made into rum in the
American
backcountry.*

A black cherry tree would have been harvested years ago for its aromatic inner bark, which would have been dried and made into cough syrup or a blood tonic tea. Today we know that only an experienced herbalist should handle the bark, as it contains cyanides that are highly toxic— especially if gathered in autumn.

distilled cherry alcohol known as kirsch. It is consumed for pleasure, but also used as a tonic for any under-the-weather feeling. Spiking cherries is another folk practice. In backwoods America, cherries macerated in a sugar-water syrup are added to brandy and allowed to cure. This makes a nice dessert topping.

Some would argue that alcohol is contradictory to herbalism. But remember that the monks of the Middle Ages, who toiled in their herb gardens, created extraordinary liqueurs (Benedictine and Chartreuse, for example) from their fragrant harvest of leaves and flowers, with which they revived the spirits of weary travelers.

To grow cherry trees, provide a moist, well-drained soil and a sunny location. The wild black cherry favors a pH of 6.5 to 7.5 and enjoys cold weather, growing especially well in zones 3 to 5. Like wild cherries, sweet cherries also like a brisk winter, but have been developed to grow in a wider range of zones, from 3 to 8. Sweet cherries need a pollinator tree; sour cherries do not. Like the apple, cherry trees bear fruit on spurs that shouldn't be removed from the tree when the fruit is picked. Prune cherry trees during the dormant season for the first two years after planting.

It's a fun experiment to try growing *P. serotina* from seed. When the fruits turn black, remove the pulp by crushing with a rolling pin. Plant the stones following the directions in Chapter 2. Cover with three inches of mulch. Or, to increase your chances of success, plant in early spring after the last frost following four months of stratification (again, see Chapter 2). The stones may have cracked slightly in the stratification process, indicating the onset of germination.

Pomegranate, *Punica granatum*

No tree is as metropolitan as the pomegranate—at least in name. This diminutive tree's genus, *Punica,* is actually the old Greek term for Carthage. Later, in Spain, the city of Granada was named for this spectacular fruit, and stone images of it are carved on the Renaissance-era Puerta de las Granadas (Gate of the Pomegranates), leading to the Alhambra.

The pomegranate is as cosmopolitan as it is metropolitan. It is a revered tree in China, its many-seeded fruits being symbols of prosperity and fertility. It is given romantic associations in the biblical Song of Solomon. In the Greek poet Homer's "Hymn to Hermes," pomegranate wood was instrumental in the discovery of fire. But even more important for the Greeks, pomegranate was considered the supreme fruit, embodying the mysteries of the rebirth of the earth each spring, as told in the myth of Demeter. Despite its exalted status, the pomegranate was also employed by the Greeks as a remedy for common tapeworm. Among medieval and Renaissance-era Europeans, pomegranate seeds were the garnish of choice. The tree was an important image in tapestries symbolizing religious events and signifying death. This symbolism became all too palpable when one considers the fate of Henry VIII's first wife, Catherine of Aragon, whose royal emblem was the pomegranate.

Over the centuries, the pomegranate has also been used as an herb. Eating the sweet seeds and juicy flesh surrounding them is certainly healthful, and you may try adding the seeds to your favorite liqueur for a custom-blended flavor. The rind is said to have astringent qualities and could therefore be worked into a skin preparation. You may consider presenting this as a challenge to your local herbalist.

The pomegranate is easier to cultivate than you think. It will grow quite well in the United States from Maryland southward and into the Southwest and California (zones 7 to 9). Though it likes a moist soil, it can withstand droughts.

Pure pomegranate juice is used to flavor dishes in the Middle East. In the west, the sweetened juice, called grenadine, is a popular flavoring and coloring for drinks.

Trees grow to about fifteen feet high or they can take on a shrub form and spread out to create a hedge.

Springtime brings a remarkable flourish of orange, red, or pinkish flowers to the pomegranate, followed by pendulous summer fruits that have an appealing clarion-shaped protrusion when immature. When obtaining stock from a nursery, be sure to specify that you want the kind that produces edible fruit and is not strictly for ornament. The former type is often grown in northern greenhouses, but industrious container cultivators have been known to produce fruit indoors (see "Special Touches," page 21).

Pomegranate bark has been used as a vermifuge in Asia and Europe. More romantically, the fruit and flower were celebrated in medieval tapestries.

A midwinter feast, Orange Chicken Breasts with Pomegranate is a fine substitute for the more usual holiday fare.

ORANGE CHICKEN BREASTS WITH POMEGRANATE

Pomegranates are just in season around the holidays, so the next time you're having a crowd over, consider this healthy, flavorful dish instead of the usual turkey or ham.

MARINADE:

1 cup freshly squeezed orange juice (about 3 large oranges)

4 tablespoons Aurum (an Italian liqueur), orange liqueur, or cognac

Grated zest of 2 oranges

$1/2$ teaspoon freshly grated nutmeg

$1/4$ teaspoon ground cardamom (optional)

6 whole boneless, skinless chicken breasts, halved

Salt and freshly ground pepper to taste

Flour for dredging

1 egg, beaten

Fine, dry bread crumbs

Olive oil

Canola oil

2 tablespoons sweet (unsalted) butter

Grated zest of 1 orange

Seeds of 1 pomegranate

Chopped Italian (flat-leaf) parsley, for garnish

Mix all marinade ingredients together in a glass bowl and marinate the chicken for at least $1/2$ hour. Drain and reserve the marinade. Pat the chicken dry with paper towels and season with salt and pepper to taste.

Dredge the breasts in flour and shake off any excess. Dip in the egg, let the excess drip off, and coat each piece with bread crumbs.

Pour equal amounts of each oil into a sauté pan to a depth of $1/4$ inch and heat on medium heat. Sauté the chicken on both sides until golden brown and cooked through, about 5 minutes per side.

Remove the chicken to a serving dish and keep warm. After all the breasts are cooked, discard the oil and add the butter, reserved marinade, and orange zest to the pan. Bring to a boil over high heat and reduce until the mixture thickens, about 3 minutes. Add the pomegranate seeds and season with salt and pepper. Pour the sauce over the chicken, sprinkle with parsley, and serve. **SERVES 6 (OR 12 AS A LIGHT MEAL)**

Joel Jason of the New York catering company In Your Kitchen contributed this recipe. See also Joel's Walnut–Wheat Berry Salad on page 73.

ENGLISH OAK, *Quercus robur*   WHITE OAK, *Quercus alba*

The mighty oak stands unchallenged at the center of the herbal grove. It is a tree without peer, worshiped and revered wherever it grows. Long a symbol of strength, the oak was sacred to both Jupiter, the supreme god of the Romans, and Thor, the Norse god of thunder. The Druids built forest altars underneath its boughs and felt that its mere presence could inspire prophecy. It was also the principal tree in rites of the summer solstice.

In northern Europe and the British Isles, when mistletoe grew in oak boughs, the powers of both were thought to be strengthened. Northern peoples have long believed that mistletoe was a protection against witchcraft. Sir J. G. Frazer, in *The Golden Bough,* wrote of a wealthy Scottish family upon whose estate grew an ancient oak. On the oak grew a profusion of mistletoe. It was thought by the local people, and by the family themselves, that their fate and fortune were tied to that of the very powerful tree. Sure enough, in later years soon after the tree died, the family fortune was lost.

The oak in question was no doubt *Quercus robur,* known commonly as the English oak. For centuries, it was used medicinally. An infusion of its astringent bark, gathered in late spring, was employed as a gargle for sore throats and was applied to cuts and burns. In North America, the white oak served the same purposes for settlers, who made a tea from the bark to wash skin irritations and to drink for stomach problems. Such practices are not recommended today because of the bark's high tannic acid content.

Growing slowly to eighty feet high, both trees do well in zones 4 to 7 and like a soil with a 6.5 to 7.5 pH. The white oak does best in a moist clay. If you want to try cultivating these oaks from seed, when acorns begin to fall off the tree, remove their caps and plant them (see "Planting from Seed," page 20). They will germinate immediately after fall sowing. Mulch beds with three inches of leaves. Remove mulch in spring.

In both North America and Europe, acorns have long served as food for both humans and animals. Native Americans would make white oak acorns into flour and roast or boil them to eat. The Miwok Indians of the West Coast used the California black oak (*Q. kelloggii*) and California white oak (*Q. lobata*) for these purposes, and were particularly keen on making acorn breads. A coffee substitute, similar to chicory and reddish in color, can be made from ground white oak acorns and is still enjoyed in parts of the South. The same could be done with English oak acorns. In Spain, English oak acorns are the sole food of the sought-after *jamón negro* pigs of Jabugo and the finest chorizos are smoked over oak wood to give them an exquisite taste. It's possible to grill at home with oak wood. Simply prune off small oak branches, dry them in the garage, cut them into chunks, and soak them in water for a half hour before barbecuing. Scatter them among the hot coals to give foods a robust, smoky flavor.

The oak leaf is also a useful part of the tree. A healthful application of the leaves has origins in eastern Europe. Oak leaves are bound together with twine and

Mistletoe grows high in an oak tree, calling to mind the legend that says that when these two plants grow together, their powers to protect against evil are strengthened. Oaks have always inspired a certain amount of respect. Indeed, John Keats called them "green-rob'd senators of mighty woods."

then used to cleanse the body with soap. Oak leaves and acorns have been used on the crest of the Cherokee Nation—symbolizing strength and permanence.

You might make fresh oak leaves into a fanciful head crown, à la Bacchus, but be aware of the implications. The Druids crowned their human sacrifices with oak leaves to make them holy to the gods. On a brighter note, the ancient Romans used oak-leaf crowns as a war decoration for any man who had saved another soldier's life in battle. Whenever he wore the crown, anyone in his presence was required to stand and pay respect. He was also granted special privileges, such as freedom from taxation and certain nasty civic duties, upon presentation of his official oak-leaf crown. All these benefits were good for a lifetime.

In England, the oak leaf has also been employed as an important symbol. Oak Apple Day, sometimes also called Royal Oak Day, commemorates the restoration of Charles II to the throne in 1660. It seems that after the Battle of Worcester, Charles fled from his pursuers (the Roundheads, supporters of Parliament who had extremely short haircuts, hence their nickname) and hid in an oak tree. From that day, the oak leaf became the Royalist badge, and was traditionally worn on one's lapel on May 29 as a patriotic gesture. The custom was practiced into this century.

This legacy of symbolic traditions prompted the United States to adopt the "oak leaf cluster" as a war decoration. Countless banks and businesses—and any company subtly attempting to establish credibility—have used the oak leaf, not to mention the acorn, as a symbol of permanence and stability. Such is the power of the oak.

AMERICAN ELDERBERRY, *Sambucus canadensis*

EUROPEAN ELDERBERRY, *Sambucus nigra*

BLUE-BERRIED ELDER, *Sambucus caerulea*

There is something about the elderberry that excites the imagination. To the Welsh, it was sacred, and a piece of the tree carried on the body was thought to cure most any ailment. Scandinavians swore by this creamy-flowered tree's prophetic powers and believed that whoever stood under it on Midsummer Eve would glimpse fairy people. Country dwellers of England once invoked the aid of this tree to compel witches to undo their spells. And in Germany, no one dared cut down an elder without first begging the tree's pardon.

As with other trees rumored to have unusual powers, the elder has inspired many medicinal uses. The inner bark, root, and leaves have been used in teas and in poultice form to banish headaches, counter edema, and cleanse wounds, to name just a few of a long list of applications. The often helpless recipient of well-intentioned treatments could actually become quite ill. This was often the preferred reaction, as elder was valued for its purgative properties. Culpeper enthused that it worked "violently." It is now understood that elder wood, root, and leaves contain potentially poisonous substances. Trained herbalists today proceed with caution; others are advised not to proceed at all.

Though traditionally associated with northern countries, the elderberry is actually one of the old herbs of Egypt. There it was used to enhance the complexion, joining a cosmetic repertoire that included kohl and henna. It is from the Egyptians that contemporary elder enthusiasts take inspiration. We now use elder-flower water as a cool wash for sunburn and add the flowers to soothing baths and skin lotions.

Delicate disks of elder flowers are also quite tasty. Come May and June, go out into the woods or your garden if you have already been smitten by this easily

Lacy elderberry flowers are not just pretty adornments. These honey-scented, creamy white flowers appear in late spring and early summer and can be made into batter-dipped fritters. They can also be infused in hot water to make a pleasant tea.

Out for a breath of fresh air, we often see ripe elderberries on woodland fringes in August and September (all the way from Nova Scotia to the Gulf of Mexico). Yet we often forget their many uses and pass them by. Remember that elderberries make extravagant pies and a delightful fruity wine.

grown tree and gather the starry-shaped blossoms in bunches. You might use them fresh in fritters, a classic presentation in which the whole flower clusters are dipped in batter, fried, and then served with a sprinkling of confectioners' sugar or a bit of cinnamon. The fresh flowers can also be broken up into smaller flowers and added to crepes and pancakes.

Even in winter, when elder branches are bare, the cupboard needn't be. The flowers can be dried for tea, so that you can evoke the taste of summer even on a snowy afternoon. The dried flowers can also be used for the aforementioned recipes, but with more restraint, because the flavor intensifies in drying. The berries, which *must* be cooked before they are used, can be made into healthful pies or preserves. They have also been made into a famous folk wine. Look for the purplish-black fruit in August and September.

Offering two seasons of harvest, a few elder trees can contribute substantial stores to the pantry and are certainly worth cultivating, especially in lean times.

European elder grows to a good thirty feet, considerably higher than its New World relative, American elder, which hovers around ten feet. The European tree is a bit more fragrant and stately, but the two species can be used interchangeably. Both favor zones 3 to 9 and like a moist soil with a bit of shade— mimicking the fringes of a woodland environment, where they grow naturally.

Elder is sometimes grown from seed. To do so, pick the ripe fruit in late summer or early autumn. Macerate with a rolling pin, and, wearing gloves, separate the seeds from the pulp. Plant seeds shallowly, according to directions in Chapter 2; mulch lightly with leaves. Be patient—your seedlings will probably not emerge until the second spring.

Despite its cosmopolitan résumé, the elder is and has always been a rustic-looking tree, so plant it in an informal setting and it is guaranteed to be at home.

Soothing Blossom Bath

The bath is an unparalleled and much overlooked delight and can have a wonderfully relaxing effect. Elder and chamomile, two calming and soothing herbs, combine in this simple half-and-half blend. This bath treatment must be created in a muslin bag or cheesecloth that can be hung around the mouth of the bath faucet. A velvet cord can be attached to form a loop.

$^1/_4$ **cup dried elder flowers** $^1/_4$ **cup dried chamomile flowers**

Dangle below bath faucet while tub is filling. After use, dry for reuse. **USE 3 TIMES**

Real ELDERBERRY JELLY

Wherever the elderberry grows wild, you'll be sure to find locals gathering pails of this exquisite fruit for jellies and jams that conjure the tastes of summer even on the most blustery winter day. Even first-time jelly makers should enjoy some success with this recipe: If it fails to jell, or "set up," after four to six weeks, it can still be used as a luscious syrup on ice cream, waffles, crepes, or anything else that goes well with a fruit topping.

3 pounds ripe elderberries, stems removed
¼ cup lemon juice
½ cup apple juice concentrate
1 1¾-ounce box fruit pectin
2 pounds sugar

Kept in a cool old-fashioned root cellar, elder preserves continue to delight all season long. They make a nice pancake dressing or waffle topping on a cold winter's morning.

Crush the berries and place them in a stainless steel or enamel saucepan. Heat on low until the magenta-colored juice begins to release. Cover and simmer for about 15 minutes.

Place the fruit in either four layers of damp cheesecloth or a jelly bag over a bowl. Grasp the ends of the jelly bag or cheesecloth and press down to extract the juice.

Measure out 2½ cups of elderberry juice and add to a nonaluminum saucepan with the lemon and apple juices. Mix in the pectin and bring the entire mixture to a hard boil. Add the sugar and return the mixture to a full boil for 1 minute, stirring constantly.

Remove from heat and skim foam. Pour at once into sterilized 8-ounce glass jars, leaving about ⅛ inch at the top. Using sterilized 2-piece lids, cover each jar, screw the bands on tightly, and invert. Let sit in a cool, dark place for 4 to 6 weeks. **MAKES ABOUT 2½ PINTS**

Elderberry expert Susie Black of Cookeville, Tennessee, introduced me to this recipe in her own farmhouse kitchen.

Sassafras, *Sassafras albidum*

Sixteenth-century Spanish adventurers in the New World didn't encounter the elusive fountain of youth, but they did find sassafras. After observing native peoples, who used root bark tea to treat fevers and other ailments, they proclaimed it to be a miracle plant. The Spaniards named the tree *Salsa frasca,* which translates roughly as "sauce of dry leaves and branches," a reference to the viscous, fragrant insides of the leaves, branches, and roots. Because of its mucilaginous—or sticky—nature, Native Americans used a twig preparation of sassafras as an eye wash, as it was thought to make foreign particles adhere to it, making it easy to flush them out. (This usage is a good example of the universal assumptions about herbal properties, as sticky clary sage seeds had been used in the same way for centuries in Europe.)

By the early seventeenth century, Jamestown colonists were turning a quick profit from sassafras. With the help of local Native Americans, they dug up the roots to obtain the bark for export to England. When it arrived in the old country, sassafras was billed as the New World wonder drug. The root bark tea was used as a treatment for colds and rheumatism. This same tea is still brewed as a spring pick-me-up by backwoods believers throughout the United States, perhaps with a price. Whether or not sassafras's apothecarial claims are apocryphal, the Federal Drug Administration has warned that safrole, a constituent of the aromatic oil found in the root bark, leaf oil, and other parts of the tree, is carcinogenic and unsafe for internal use. This also means that sassafras root is no longer used in root beer, though it was once the principal ingredient. The one surviving use of sassafras was actually a Native American invention: They used the young leaves to thicken foods. Today it is called filé and is used to thicken New Orleans–style gumbo.

Sassafras is fit to grow in the herbal grove for its looks alone. The distinctive leaves take on a mitten, oval, or more symmetrically lobed form. In autumn, the tree is especially outstanding, turning crimson and sometimes yellow. Its

Sassafras's perky, often mitten-like leaves easily identify it in spring—come autumn, look for a magnificent golden, orange, crimson, and (sometimes) pink foliage. In its heyday in Colonial America, sassafras root bark was exported to Europe for use as a medicinal tea.

Fresh springtime sassafras leaves have the invigorating scent so common to members of the Laurel family, such as bay and cinnamon. The mucilaginous leaves are pulverized and made into filé powder used as a basis for soup stocks, especially New Orleans gumbo.

the tree is especially outstanding, turning crimson and sometimes yellow. Its blue autumnal berries, loved by birds, are carried on bright red stalks. Sassafras is especially at home on the edge of a woodland setting, in full sun to light shade, and thrives among its own kind in a moist, acidic soil. It is suited to zones 4 to 8. You can grow sassafras from seed by picking the mature dark blue fruits in late summer or early autumn. Remove seeds by crushing fruits with a rolling pin. Following directions in Chapter 2, stratify the seeds during the winter, beginning four months prior to planting. Sow in spring after the last frost.

An herbal woodland garden could include sassafras with other low-growing, shade-loving herbs, such as lady's mantle, European ginger, violets, goldenseal, and mayapple. Sassafras will grow to about fifty feet, and will give your backyard a woodsy, country look.

ROWAN, *Sorbus aucuparia* MOUNTAIN ASH, *Sorbus americana*

In the triumvirate of sacred grove trees, the red-berried rowan blazes brightly alongside the ancient oak and gleaming birch. It is said to be one of the world's most empowered trees. The color red has long been associated with magic, and this is one possible reason that the rowan inspires reverence. The other explanation may be that this beautiful tree works magic in the herbal pharmacy.

Centuries ago in France and Germany, branches of rowan, sometimes called European mountain ash, were brought indoors for protection against lightning. In the Scandinavian countries, the rowan's name, *Runn* or *Runa*, means "rune," indicating magical associations. In the seventh book of his remarkable *The Golden Bough*, Sir J. G. Frazer wrote of the Scandinavian belief that the "flying rowan"—one that has taken root in an off-the-ground place, such as in a narrow space between two rocks on a cliff or even among the roots of another tree—was supremely powerful. Walking sticks, divining rods, and farm implements made from such a tree were considered potent protectors.

In Scotland, the rowan was once considered *the* protection against witchcraft, whether hung over the hearth as a reassurance, placed in the barn to shield cattle from evil, or carried by people in the form of two twigs fashioned into a cross and knotted with red thread. It was believed that the tree couldn't be touched by "unholy fingers," as a Dr. Jamieson reported in Hilderic Friend's *Flower Lore*. Following this reasoning, planting a rowan near one's cottage was also a useful, all-purpose protectant.

As with holly, pine, and other herbal trees that figured so prominently in pagan rituals, the rowan became sanctified in Christianity as well. That is why the tree is so often found today growing in churchyards of both the British Isles and the United States.

The rowan's reputation is not built on looks alone. At the same time the tree was revered for its magical associations, it had long been used in European herbalism for its healthful berries. This tradition continues in North America, where a tree known as both the rowan and the mountain ash grows. American herbalist Ryan Drum, Ph.D., who lives on Waldron Island off the coast of Washington State, recognizes the long tradition of *Sorbus* and uses American mountain ash as both a stimulating food and medicine. In his region, the berries ripen anywhere from the first of August until the end of September, depending on local sun and temperature. In late summer, Dr. Drum watches and waits until the berries are plump and juicy, a dark reddish orange, and have an exquisite taste that balances both tart and sweet. He notices, however, that local birds are also vigilant and sample rowan berries regularly to see if they are ripe. On several occasions the birds stripped virtually all the berrries from a tree early the same morning that Dr. Drum was planning to do the same. To beat the birds, he sometimes harvests not totally ripe berries and uses them "with perfectly acceptable results." He recommends cutting the berry clusters to save the woody stubs of the fruiting spurs. This can be practiced on both the rowan and the American mountain ash.

Dr. Drum's favorite *Sorbus* recipe accompanies this section. Fresh rowan juice has been used as a soothing gargle and the vitamin-rich juice is also a pleasant drink.

With so many uses and potential magical benefits to boot, there are only two possible reasons *not* to grow rowan: it might not thrive in your area (it's happiest in zones 2 to 7), and, as Dr. Jamieson cautioned, your fingers could be deemed "unholy." An acid, well-drained soil will encourage rowan to grow, possibly to fifty feet. If you want to grow rowan from seed, pick the ripe fruits in late summer or early autumn. Crush with a rolling pin and extract the seeds by hand. Sow according to directions in Chapter 2, covering with peat moss or leaves.

Growing in a churchyard, a magnificent specimen of rowan may well have been planted because of superstitions surrounding the tree's protective powers. Indeed, farmers once hung sprays of rowan berries from barn rafters to protect cattle from "demons" at night.

Honied Rowan Berries

Here is a wonderful recipe for honied rowan berries that can be eaten alone by the spoonful, or used in pie fillings and even as a meat glaze. A heaping spoonful can also be mixed with hot water to make a refreshing winter drink.

Keep in mind, too, that fresh rowan berries served with fine vanilla ice cream are a treat, though some people may find them a little sour. They can also be dried and used as an alternative to raisins. They'll keep for years in a sealed jar.

EQUAL PARTS:

Clover honey   **Rowan berries**

Heat clover honey to 180 degrees Fahrenheit. Add crushed, cleaned rowan berries. Strain to remove stems. Seal in sterilized canning jars for at least 3 months in a warm place (80 to 100 degrees Fahrenheit). Store in the refrigerator when not using.

Dr. Ryan Drum, herbalist of Waldron Island, Washington, provided this recipe.

SOURCES

NURSERIES

Applesource
Route 1
Chapin, IL 62628
(217) 245-7589
Neither a nursery nor a culinary source, this educational organization provides Sampler Packs of 12 antique apple varieties and Explorer Packs of 6 varieties (2 types of each) at harvest time; free catalog.

Arbor & Espalier
201 Buena Vista Avenue East
San Francisco, CA 94117
(415) 626-8880
Espalier-trained apple trees; trellis-trained pears, pomegranates, persimmons, and stone fruit; catalog $1.

The Banana Tree
715 Northampton Street
Easton, PA 18042
(610) 253-9589
Seeds of rare trees—cinnamon, allspice, eucalyptus—for experienced growers; catalog $3.

Chestnut Hill Nursery
Route 1, Box 341
Alachua, FL 32615
(904) 462-2820
Fruit and nut crops, including cold-hardy figs, blight-resistant chestnut trees, and kaki persimmons; free catalog.

Dabney Herbs
Box 22061
Louisville, KY 40252
(502) 893-5198
Osage orange, eucalyptus, Kentucky coffee tree, persimmon, sassafras; also sells Olive Oil Soap, Sweet Almond Oil, and potpourri supplies, including orange flowers, olive leaves, myrrh, frankincense, sassafras root bark, and cinnamon chips and sticks; catalog $2.

Earth Advocates
Adam and Sue Turtle
Route 3, Box 624
Livingston, TN 38570-9547
Land-use consultants with extensive nursery of woody plants.

Edible Landscaping
P.O. Box 77
Afton, VA 22920
(804) 361-9134
Mulberries, jujubes, pawpaws, and more; free catalog.

Exotica Rare Fruit Nursery
P.O. Box 160
Vista, CA 92083
(619) 724-9093
Retail nursery address: 2508 #B,
East Vista Way, Vista, CA
A constantly evolving collection of seeds and rooted cuttings of many unusual fruit and nut trees from the tropics and subtropics; examples include allspice,

olive, banana, carob, fig, persimmon, Japanese raisin, mulberry, pinyon pine, Italian stone pine, jojoba, date palm, baobab, and chicle (chewing gum tree); free catalog.

The Flowery Branch
P.O. Box 1330
Flowery Branch, GA 30542
(404) 536-8380
Seeds of a variety of hard-to-find trees, including camphor, lemon, Japanese bitter orange, eucalyptus, Osage orange, Southern bayberry, California pepper, Brazilian pepper, Australian tea, and bay (laurel); catalog $3, refundable with first order.

Four Winds Growers
P.O. Box 3538
Fremont, CA 94539
(510) 656-2591
Retail nursery address: 42186 Palm Avenue, Fremont, CA
Dwarf and standard citrus varieties—orange, lemon, grapefruit, lime, kumquat—shipped bare-root (unable to ship to TX, FL, AZ) booklet entitled "How to Grow" available with SASE and .32-cent stamp.

Gilbertie's Herb Gardens
7 Sylvan Lane
Westport, CT 06880
(203) 227-4175
Bay trees.

Hicks Nursery
100 Jericho Turnpike
Westbury, LI 11590
(516) 334-0066
Wide variety of trees, with occasional citrus; retail only but worth the trip.

Hidden Springs Nursery
Route 14, Box 159
Cookeville, TN 38501
(615) 268-9889
Fascinating selection of diverse trees, including autumn olive, sea buckthorn, and edible honeysuckle.

Hopkins Nursery
5200 S.W. 160 Ave. (Dykes Road)
Fort Lauderdale, FL 33331
(305) 434-5558
Citrus and rare fruit trees; free catalog.

Lake County Nursery Inc.
Route 84, Box 122
Perry, OH 44081-0122
(216) 259-5571
Balsam fir, maples, serviceberries, quince, dogwoods, Kentucky coffee tree, sweetgum, witch hazels, and magnolia; wholesale only through garden centers and landscapers.

Lakeshore Tree Farms
Box 2A, RR #3
Saskatoon, SK
Canada
S7K 3J6
(306) 382-2077
Cold-hardy fruit trees; catalog $2.

Lamtree Farm
Route 1, Box 162
2323 Copeland Road
Warrensville, NC 28693
White oak, Chinese dogwood, spicebush, and more.

Henry Leuthardt Nurseries
Montauk Highway
P.O. Box 666
East Moriches, NY 11940
(516) 878-1387
Espaliered, dwarf, and semidwarf fruit trees (apple, pear, plum, cherry, peach, nectarine, apricot); free catalog.

Logee's Greenhouses
141 North Street
Danielson, CT 06239
(203) 774-8038
Citrus and fig among the rare-plant selection; catalog $3.

Long Hungry Creek Nursery
Jeff Poppen
Red Boiling Springs, TN 37150
Specializes in disease-resistant apple trees.

Lychee Tree Nursery
3151 S. Kanner Highway
Stuart, FL 34994
(407) 283-4054
Mulberry and assorted tropical fruit trees; retail only.

Mellinger's
2310 West South Range Road
North Lima, OH 44452-9731
(216) 549-9861
(800) 321-7444
Dogwood, pinyon pine, juniper, ginkgo (males only), rowan, coffee tree (seed only), black birch, maple, linden, apples, peaches, hardy almond, black and English walnut, Nut Tree Collection packs; free catalog.

Northwind Nursery and Orchards
7910 335th Avenue N.W.
Princeton, MN 55371
(612) 389-4920
Apples and mulberries among a selection of organically grown trees; catalog $1.

Owen Farms
2951 Curve-Nankipoo Road
Route #3, Box #158-A
Ripley, TN 38063
(901) 635-1588
Redbud, 40 varieties of dogwood, 6 varieties of witch hazel, 40 varieties of maple, and sourwood; catalog $2.

Pacific Tree Farms
4301 Lynwood Drive
Chula Vista, CA 91910
(619) 422-2400
Many unusual fruit-bearing trees, along with herbal favorites jojoba, low-chill apple, peach, cinnamon, Neem tree, and fig; catalog $2.

Raintree Nursery
391 Butts Road
Morton, WA 98356
(206) 496-6400
Citrus, fig, pomegranate, apple, pear, peach, black walnut, and other nut-bearing trees; free catalog.

Renaissance Acres
4450 Valentine
Whitmore Lake, MI 48189
(313) 449-8336
Organic herb farm carrying bay and ginkgo; free brochure with SASE; catalog $2.

Sonoma Antique Apple Nursery
4395 Westside Road
Healdsburg, CA 95448
(707) 433-6420
Excellent apple tree source; free catalog.

Southmeadow Fruit Gardens
Lakeside, MI 49116
(616) 469-2865
Unusual apple varieties, including cider, extrahardy, and orchard types; autumn olive; peaches; plums; cherries; quinces; medlars; price list is free; catalog with fascinating history of varieties is $9 post-paid.

Stark Brothers Nurseries
Louisiana, MO 63353
(800) 325-4180
Variety of fruit and nut trees, including peaches, apples, cherries, and black and English walnuts; free catalog.

Well-Sweep Herb Farm
205 Mount Bethel Road
Port Murray, NJ 07865
(908) 852-5390
Numerous unusual herbal trees, including cinnamon and frankincense; catalog $2.

Gardens to Visit

Arnold Arboretum of Harvard University
The Arbor Way
Jamaica Plain, MA 02130
(617) 524-1718
Vast selection of trees; adult's and children's education programs teaching such skills as tree propagation.

Atlanta Botanical Garden
P.O. Box 77246
Atlanta, GA 30357
(404) 876-5859
Interesting selection of Southern trees.

Boscobel
Route 9D
Garrison, NY 10524
(914) 265-3638
Orangerie and quince and apple orchard.

Boyce Thompson Southwestern Arboretum
37615 East Highway 60
Superior, AZ 85273
(602) 689-2723
Fragrant, towering red-gum eucalyptus grove.

The Cloisters/Medieval Herb Garden
Fort Tryon Park
New York, NY 10040
(212) 233-3700
Trio of courtyard gardens in medieval style.

Colonial Pennsylvania Plantations
Ridley Creek State Park
Media, PA 19063
(215) 566-1725
Colonial herb gardens and orchard of antique fruits.

Dawes Arboretum
7770 Jacksontown Road S.E.
Newark, OH 43056-9380
(614) 323-2355
Educational maple, oak, and holly trails, including late winter maple-syrup tours; fall pruning workshops; "Arbor Day for Everyone" celebration.

Des Moines Botanical Center
909 East River Drive
Des Moines, IA 50316
(515) 242-2934
Herbal shrubs and trees.

Fairchild Tropical Gardens
10901 Old Cutler Road
Miami, FL 33156-4296
(305) 667-1651
Narrated tram tours; plant information line.

Ginkgo Petrified Forest State Park & the
    Wanapum Recreation Area
P.O. Box 1203
Vantage, WA 98950
(509) 856-2700
Fascinating "Trees of Stone" interpretive trail with fossilized wood specimens, including ginkgo, maple, Douglas fir, spruce, walnut, and elm.

Israel Crane House Gardens
Montclair Historical Society
108 Orange Road
Montclair, NJ 07042
(201) 744-1796
Eighteenth-century–style plantings include old-fashioned trees.

J. Paul Getty Museum
17985 Pacific Coast Highway
Malibu, CA 90265
(310) 458-2003
Ancient Roman villa–style garden with apple, fig, citrus, bay, and myrtle.

Lake of the Woods (Mabery Gelvin)
    Botanic Gardens
P.O. Box 1040
Mahomet, IL 61853
(217) 586-4630
Woodland trails; visitors are provided with information sheets on trees and other plants and their historic uses.

Los Angeles State and County
    Arboretum
301 North Baldwin Avenue
Arcadia, CA 91007
(818) 821-3222
Many herbal trees, including eucalyptus and bay.

Minnesota Landscape Arboretum
3675 Arboretum Drive
Chanhassen, MN 55317-0039
(612) 443-2460
Horticultural Research Center has introduced more than 70 cold-hardy fruit varieties since 1967; garden tours, classes, and special events.

Mission Gardens of California (many of the missions gardens, dating from the eighteenth and early nineteenth centuries, contain original trees planted by the Franciscans or descendants of those trees):

Carmel Mission
P.O. Box 2235
Carmel, CA 93921
(408) 624-1271
Mediterranean cork oak and Indian fig among highlights.

Mission Gardens of California (cont.)

La Purisima Mission State Park
2295 Purisima Road
Lompoc, CA 93436
(805) 733-1303
Century-old olive groves, Mission fig, pomegranate, citrus, cottonwood (poplar), Southern California black walnut, and European myrtle; educational programs.

San Diego Misson
901 Camino del Rio South
San Diego, CA 92108
(619) 543-9000
Antique olive grove.

San Fernando Rey de Espana Mission
15151 San Fernando Mission
    Boulevard
Mission Hills, CA 91345
(818) 361-0186
Olives and palms among plantings.

San Juan Capistrano Mission
P.O. Box 697
San Juan Capistrano, CA 92693
(714) 248-2048
Mexican elderberry, buckthorn, and California walnut.

Santa Barbara Mission
2201 Laguna Street
Santa Barbara, CA 93105
(805) 682-4713
Grand old fig tree and loquat.

Santa Clara Mission/Santa Clara
    University
Attn: Visitor Center
500 El Camino Real, Box 3217
Santa Clara, CA 95053-3217
(408) 554-4023
Olives, date palm, yew, citrus, and others.

Morris Arboretum
9414 Meadowbrook Avenue
Philadelphia, PA 19118
(215) 247-5777
Extensive collection of labeled trees and shrubs; guided and self-guided tours of blossoming trees and medicinal plants; courses offered on arboriculture; telephone plant clinic.

New York Botanical Garden
Southern Boulevard and 200th Street
Bronx, New York 10458
(718) 817-8705
Beautiful tree-filled grounds; plant information line.

Royal Botanical Gardens
P.O. Box 399
Hamilton, ON
Canada
LAN 3H8
(905) 527-1158
Nice selection of cold-climate species.

State Arboretum of Virginia
P.O. Box 175
Boyce, VA 22620
(703) 837-1758
Diverse collection of Southern trees.

State of New Hampshire Urban Forestry Center
45 Elwyn Road
Portsmouth, NH 03801
(603) 431-6774
Forested areas and small arboretum with variety of species as well as herb garden.

Strybing Arboretum & Botanical Gardens
Ninth Avenue and Lincoln Way
San Francisco, CA 94122
(415) 753-7089
Variety of species that thrive on West Coast.

U.S. National Arboretum
3501 New York Avenue N.E.
Washington, DC 20002
(202) 245-2726
Arboretum of North American trees, featuring hollies, conifers, and bonsai conservatory; special events; propagation workshops.

HEALING, COSMETIC, AND HOUSEHOLD PRODUCTS

Aphrodisia
264 Bleecker Street
New York, NY 10014
(212) 989-6440
Extensive potpourri and incense selection, among many other products.

Belle Epoque
Box 461
Ayer's Cliff
Quebec, Canada JOB1CO
(819) 838-5688
Almond soap; magnolia perfume oil; sweet almond massage oil, and more; gift baskets available.

Body Elements
3320 North Third Street
Arlington, VA 22201-1712
(703) 525-0585
Array of natural products, including almond cream, piñon pine soap, and bark-, leaf-, and berry-based herbal formulas.

Erbe
196 Prince Street
New York, NY 10012
(212) 966-1445
(800) 432-ERBE
Sweet almond oil. Free catalog.

The Excelsior Incense Works
1413 Van Dyke Avenue
San Francisco, CA 94124
(415) 822-9124
Rare and unusual incenses, resins, and gums from around the world, including frankincense and myrrh; also provides incense-making supplies.

Green Terrestrial
P.O. Box 266
Milton, NY 12547
(914) 795-5238
Wildcrafted herbal products, including olive-oil–based massage oils and ginkgo tincture; free catalog.

Hearts o' Flowers
Barbara R. Duncan, Ph.D.
80 Lakeside Drive
Franklin, NC 28734
All-natural perfume creams made from herbs: Carolina allspice, frankincense and myrrh, clary sage, mint, rose geranium, and others; send SASE for flyer.

Island Herbs
Wildcrafted & Organically Grown Medicinal Herbs
Ryan Drum, Ph.D.
Waldron Island, WA 98297-9999
High-quality bulk herbs, including alder bark, balm of Gilead buds, wild cherry bark, hawthorn flowers and berries, rowan berries, and willow bark; herbal retreat available; closed Dec. 20–Feb. 20.

Kiehl's
109 Third Avenue
New York, NY 10003
(212) 677-3171
(212) 475-3698
(800) KIEHLS-1
Many herbal-based bath and cosmetic
products, including Milk, Honey and
Almond Scrub; Myrrh Essence; Cherry
Blossom Essence; Tangerine Essence;
and Siberian Pine Needle Oil.

Jas. Kirkland
Kirkland's Wood
Swainsboro, GA 30401
Fanciful products scented with herbs;
Harvest Line features woodland
collages; wholesale only—write for
nearest store location.

Loom Co.
26 W. 17th Street
New York, NY 10011
(212) 366-7214
Natural Orange box (made from dried
citrus peel) and Stolen Flowers line of
herb-filled bottles; wholesale only—
write for nearest store location.

Lunar Farms Herbal Specialists
#3 Highland-Greenhills
Gilmer, TX 75644
(903) 734-5893
Certified organic Magic Cream Comfrey
Salve, with pure essential orange oil;
instruction; spring herb festival; send
SASE for brochure.

Meadowbrook Herb Garden Catalog
93 Kingstown Road
Wyoming, RI 02898
(401) 539-0209
Fragrance oils include bay leaf,
cedarwood, clove bud, eucalyptus,
juniper berry, myrrh, pine needle,
sassafras, and tea tree; Citrus Body Oil
and Pine Bath Oil; various organic and
wildcrafted herbs; also includes culinary
mixtures, such as cinnamon sticks, bay
leaves, cloves, and juniper berries.

Mountain Rose Herbs
P.O. Box 2000
Redway, CA 95560
(707) 923-3941
fax: (707) 923-7867
Neroli facial oil; almond facial scrub;
citrus cleansing grains; throat soother
with slippery elm; ginkgo/skullcap
extract; essential oils of tea tree,
eucalyptus, and cedarwood; catalog $1.

Native Scents, Inc.
212 Camino de la Merced
P.O. Box 5639
Taos, NM 87571
(505) 758-9656
Cedar, juniper, and piñon incense wands;
piñon resin incense. Free catalog.

Nature's Apothecary
6350 Gunpark Drive
Suite 500
Boulder, CO 80301
(303) 581-0288
(800) 999-7422
Aromatherapy blends and pure essences
include bay, eucalyptus, cedar, lemon,
orange, sandalwood, and frankincense;
fresh plant extracts include wild cherry
bark, white oak bark, and juniper; free
catalog.

Real Goods
966 Mazzoni Street
Ukiah, CA 95482
(800) 762-7325
Catalog of earth-aware items includes
tree-related household products; free
catalog.

Swissette Herb Farm
Clove Road
Salisbury Mills, NY 12577
(914) 496-7841
fax: (914) 496-3790
Herbal teas include tree-based varieties.

Tenzing Momo, Inc.
93 Pike Place Market
Seattle, WA 98101
(206) 623-9837
Bulk herbs, Chinese medicines,
essential oils, and sun-dried herbs; send
SASE for brochure.

Woodland Essence
P.O. Box 206
Cold Brook, NY 13324
Tree-based tinctures, massage oils, and
salves; pine-needle baskets; workshops
in tree identification and wildcrafting.

Wyoming Wildcrafters
P.O. Box 3876
Jackson, WY 83001
(307) 733-6731
Wildcrafted and organic botanicals,
including chokecherry, willow, black
walnut, and prickly ash; free catalog.

CULINARY PRODUCTS

Aeppler Orchard
Oconomowoc, WI 53066
(414) 567-6635
Apple syrups; price list available.

Almond Plaza
P.O. Box 426
Maumee, OH 43537
(800) 225-NUTS
Fresh nuts through the California
Almond Growers Association; free
catalog.

Bainbridge Corporation
P.O. Box 587
White Bluff, TN 37187
(615) 797-4547
(800) 545-9205
Black-Walnut Jelly for spreading and
baking; fig preserves.

Callaway Gardens
Pine Mountain, GA 31822
(706) 633-2251 (ask for Country Store)
Genuine Georgia peach preserves and
peach butter.

Cherry Hill Cooperative Cannery Inc.
291 Barre-Montpelier Road
Barre, VT 05641
(802) 479-2558
(800) 468-3020
Apple butters, maple syrup, and maple-
syrup–sweetened applesauces.

Chestnut Hill Orchards
3300 Bee Cave Road
Suite 650
Austin, TX 78746-6663
(512) 477-3020
Chestnut products.

Crane Orchards and Pie Pantry
6054 124th Avenue
Fennville, MI 49408
(616) 561-2297
Apple and cherry pies, apple-walnut
cakes; free brochure.

Dymple's Delight
Route 4, Box 53
Mitchell, IN 47446
(812) 849-3487
Persimmon Pulp, canned or frozen, for
use in puddings and other desserts; price
list available.

Gazin's
P.O. Box 19221, Dept. HG
New Orleans, LA 70179
to request catalog, $2, refunded with
    first order: (504) 482-0302
for orders only: (800) 262-6410
Sassafras-based gumbo filé.

Green Shutters Specialty Foods
P.O. Box 564
Clayton, GA 30525
(706) 782-3342
(800) 535-5971
Wild Crabapple Jelly, Fig Jam, Georgia
Peach Jam, Apple Butter, Peach and
Pecan Preserves, Georgia Mountain
Sourwood Honey, Cinnamon Biscuit
Mix; gift baskets available; free catalog.

Lester Farms
4317 Margaret Lane
Winters, CA 95694
(916) 795-2693
Dried fruits and nuts; gift packs
available; write for brochure.

The Linden Beverage Company
Route 1, Box 35
Linden, VA 22642
(703) 635-2118
(800) 462-1867
Alpenglow Apple Cider; wholesale only;
also runs retail store, The Apple House.

McFadden Farm
Potter Valley, CA 95469
(707) 743-1122
(800) 544-8230
Bay leaves for the spice rack; ornamental
bay-leaf wreaths; write for price list.

Missouri Dandy Pantry
414 North Street
Stockton, MO 65785
(417) 276-5121
(800) 872-6879
Black walnuts, cashews, pistachios, and
other nuts; nut-filled candies and gifts;
free catalog.

Nichols Garden Nursery
1190 North Pacific
Albany, OR 97321
(503) 928-9280
Primarily a seed source of rare edibles
and herbs, but also offers culinary
products, including dried whole-leaf bay;
cinnamon sticks; cinnamon, lemon, and
orange essential oils; linden flower tea;
cherry bark teas; also, oils for fragrance
include eucalyptus, fir needle, and
myrrh; potpourri ingredients include
myrrh gum, frankincense tears, lemon
and orange peel, orange flowers; free
catalog.

Rent Mother Nature
52 New Street
P.O. Box 193
Cambridge, MA 02238
(617) 354-5430
Maple, peach, apple, tangelo
(honeybell), grapefruit, and Nicaraguan
coffee trees can be "rented" for their
syrups, fruits, and beans; various gift
plans available; free catalog ($3 in
Canada).

St. Clair Ice Cream Company USA
140 Hanford Place
South Norwalk, CT 06854
(203) 853-4774
Ships ice cream fruits or sorbets in
maple-walnut, lemon, peach, and other
flavors; send for brochure.

Santa Barbara Olive Company
P.O. Box 1570
Santa Ynez, CA 93460
(805) 688-9917
(800) 624-4896
Marinated, spiced, and stuffed black and
green olives and specialty oils and salad
dressings in gift boxes.

Señor Murphy Candymaker
P.O. Box 2505
Santa Fe, NM 87504-2505
(505) 988-4311
Locally grown piñones (pine nuts),
roasted and salted, as well as used in
candy, such as Piñon Brittle; pecans and
almonds also available; free catalog.

Shields Date Gardens
80-225 Highway 111
Indio, CA 92201
(619) 347-0996
Fresh dates and date cake; citrus; dried
fruits also available; write for brochure.

Spiceland Inc.
3206 North Major
Chicago, IL 60634
(312) 736-1000
(800) 352-8671
Bay leaf, cinnamon sticks; free catalog.

Sugarbush Farm Syrup
R.F.D. 1, Box 568
Woodstock, VT 05091
(802) 457-1757
Maple syrup; free catalog.

Vanns Spices
1238 East Joppa Road
Baltimore, MD 21286
(410) 583-1643
Cinnamon sticks, French mulling spices
(including orange peel and juniper
berries), almond and lemon oils, peach
essence, and sassafras-based gumbo filé
among goods; free catalog.

Walnut Acres
Penns Creek, PA 17862
(800) 433-3998
Organically grown and healthy foods,
including nuts with herbal applications;
free catalog.

SOCIETIES, PROGRAMS, AND PROFESSIONAL ORGANIZATIONS

American Association of Nurserymen
1250 Eye Street N.W.
Suite 500
Washington, DC 20005
(202) 789-2900
fax: (202) 789-1893
National trade association representing
the nursery industry; also has state
associations; Horticultural Research
Institute comprises one division; call or
write for information, referrals, or
brochures.

American Botanical Council
P.O. Box 201660
Austin, TX 78720
(512) 331-8868
Nonprofit organization copublishes
scientific journal, *The Herbalgram,* with
Herb Research Foundation; publishes
booklets on specific herbs.

American Pomological Society
Penn State
103 Tyson Building
University Park, PA 16802
Dedicated to fruit growing.

American Society of Consulting
    Arborists
700 Canterbury Road
Clearwater, FL 34624

Arnold Arboretum of Harvard University
125 Arbor Way
Jamaica Plain, MA 02130
(617) 524-1718 (event line)
(617) 495-2633 (education)
Workshops in pruning, identifying trees,
and selecting trees for the home
landscape.

Famous & Historic Trees
8555 Plummer Road
Jacksonville, FL 32219
(800) 677-0727
Program committed to creating historic
groves in American communities; Tree
Selection Catalog available, organized by
trees with historic, literary, and other
themes, as well as according to species;
each tree offered is progeny or offspring
of the original famous or historic tree.

Herb Research Foundation
1007 Pearl Street
Boulder, CO 80302
(303) 449-2265
Source of information on herbal
medicinal uses.

Herb Society of America
9019 Kirtland Chardon Road
Kirtland, OH 44094
(216) 256-0514
Write for information on memberships.

International Golden Fossil Tree Society
201 West Graham Avenue
Lombard, IL 60148
Dedicated to the ginkgo; write for
membership details.

International Herb Association
1202 Allanson Road
Mundelein, IL 60060
(708) 949-4372

International Oak Society
Steven Roesch
14870 Kingsway Drive
New Berlin, WI 53151
Oak appreciation society dedicated to
placing more species under cultivation;
free seed exchange; to receive the IOS
journal ($10 for 2 issues), write to:

International Society of Arboriculture
P.O. Box GG
Savoy, IL 61874
(217) 355-9411
Nonprofit organization supporting tree-
care research around the world and
dedicated to the care and preservation of
ornamental trees; write for tree-care
pamphlets.

Carol McGrath
3730 Press Avenue
Victoria, BC
Canada
V8X 2Z1
Tours of herbal trees; instruction in
making salves and tinctures.

North American Fruit Explorers
Route 1, Box 94
Chapin, IL 62628
Publishes *Pomona,* a quarterly journal;
members gain access to extensive
NAFEX library; write for membership
information.

Northern Nut Growers Association
Ken Bauman, treasurer
9870 South Palmer Road
New Carlisle, OH 45344
(513) 878-2610
Write for membership details.

Rare Pit and Plant Council
c/o Debbie Peterson
251 West 11th Street
New York, NY 10014
Newsletter available on growing unusual
plants indoors; write for subscription
rates.

Smoky Mountain Field School
Univ. of Tennessee
600 Henley Street
Suite 105
Knoxville, TN 37902
(615) 974-0150
(800) 284-8885
Wilderness skills and appreciation
program; areas of instruction include
foraging in Great Smoky Mountains
National Park and native plant
propagation; write for brochure.

Tropical Flowering Tree Society
Dolores Fugina
Fairchild Tropical Gardens
10901 Old Cutler Road
Miami, FL 33156-4296
(305) 248-0818
Write for membership information.

BIBLIOGRAPHY

HISTORIC AND CONTEMPORARY WESTERN HERBALISM

Bremness, Lesley. *The Complete Book of Herbs*. New York: Viking Penguin, 1988.

Culpeper, Nicholas. *Culpeper's Complete Herball*. Secaucus, N.J.: Chartwell Books, 1985.

Gerard, John. *Herball*. Arranged by Marcus Woodward. New York: Dover Publications, 1969.

Lust, John. *The Herb Book*. New York: Bantam Books, 1983.

Wigginton, Eliot, ed. *Foxfire 3*. Garden City, N.Y.: Doubleday Books, 1975.

NATIVE AMERICAN HERBALISM

Densmore, Frances. *How Indians Use Wild Plants for Food, Medicine, & Crafts*. New York: Dover Publications, 1974.

Kavasch, Barrie. *Native Harvests: Recipes and Botanicals of the American Indian*. New York: Random House, 1979.

Mooney, James. *Myths and Legends of the Cherokee*. Nashville: Charles Elder, 1978.

Vogel, Virgil J. *American Indian Medicine*. Norman, Okla.: University of Oklahoma Press, 1970.

FOLKLORIC AND MAGICAL USAGES

Brier, Bob. *Ancient Eyptian Magic*. New York: William Morrow, 1980.

Cunningham, Scott. *Cunningham's Encyclopedia of Magical Herbs*. St. Paul, Minn.: Llewellyn Publications, 1990.

Fielder, Mildred. *Plant Medicine and Folklore*. New York: Winchester Press, 1975.

Frazer, Sir James George. *The Golden Bough: A Study in Magic and Religion, Part VII, Vol. II*. New York: St. Martin's Press, 1966.

Friend, Hilderic. *Flower Lore*. Rockport, Mass.: Pararesearch, 1981.

Hand, Wayland D. *Magical Medicine: The Folkloric Component of Medicine in the Folk Belief, Custom, and Ritual of the Peoples of Europe and America*. Berkeley, Calif.: University of California Press, 1980.

GENERAL REFERENCE

Dick, William B. *Dick's Encyclopedia of Practical Receipts and Processes, or How They Did It in the 1870s*. New York: Funk & Wagnalls, n.d.

Lewis, Naphtali, and Meyer Reinhold. *Roman Civilization, Sourcebook II: The Empire*. New York: Harper & Row, 1966.

Root, Waverley. *Food: An Authoritative Visual History and Dictionary of the Foods of the World.* New York: Simon and Schuster, 1980.

GARDENING AND GARDEN HISTORY

Coats, Alice, M. *The Plant Hunters.* New York: McGraw-Hill, 1969.

Davis, Brian. *The Gardener's Illustrated Encyclopedia of Trees and Shrubs.* Emmaus, Pa.: Rodale, 1987.

Dirr, Michael. *Manual of Woody Landscape Plants: Their Identification, Ornamental Characteristics, Culture, Propagation, and Uses.* 3rd ed. Champaign, Ill.: Stikes Publishing Co., 1983.

Hedrick, U.P. *A History of Horticulture in America to 1860.* New York: Oxford University Press, 1950.

Huxley, Anthony. *An Illustrated History of Gardening.* New York: Paddington Press Ltd., 1978.

Kremer, Bruno P. *Árboles (Trees).* Barcelona: Editorial blume, S.A., 1986.

McLean, Teresa. *Medieval English Gardens.* New York: Viking, 1980.

Phipps, Frances. *Colonial Kitchens, Their Furnishings and Their Gardens.* New York: Hawthorn Books, 1972.

United States Department of Agriculture/Forest Service. *Seeds of Woody Plants in the United States.* Agriculture Handbook No. 450. Washington, D.C.: U.S. Government Printing Office, 1989.

FORAGING, USE, AND IDENTIFICATION

Angell, Madeline. *A Field Guide to Berries and Berrylike Fruits.* New York: Bobbs-Merrill Co., 1981.

Berglund, Berndt, and Clare E. Bolsby. *The Edible Wild.* New York: Charles Scribner's Sons, 1971.

Bringle Clarke, Charlotte. *Edible and Useful Plants of California.* Berkeley, Calif.: University of California Press, 1977.

Foster, Steven, *Ginkgo.* Austin, Texas: American Botanical Council, 1991.

——— and Duke, James A. *Peterson Field Guide to Medicinal Plants of Eastern and Central North America.* Boston: Houghton Mifflin, 1990.

Gibbons, Euell. *Stalking the Wild Asparagus.* New York: David McKay Co., 1962.

Jordan, Michael. *A Guide to Wild Plants: The Edible and Poisonous Species of the Northern Hemisphere.* London: Millington Books, 1976.

Knutsen, Karl. *Wild Plants You Can Eat: A Guide to Identification and Preparation.* Garden City, N.Y.: Doubleday & Co., 1975.

Little, Elbert L. *The Audubon Society Field Guide to North American Trees (Eastern Region).* New York: Knopf, 1989.

———. *The Audubon Society Field Guide to North American Trees (Western Region).* New York: Knopf, 1990.

Preston, Richard J., Jr. *North American Trees.* 3rd ed. Cambridge, Mass.: MIT Press, 1976.

INDEX

About the Author

Mary Forsell is the author of *Heirloom Herbs: Using Old-Fashioned Herbs in Gardens, Recipes, and Decorations* (Villard, 1990), *Berries: Cultivation, Decoration, and Recipes* (Bantam, 1989), and *The Book of Flower Arranging* (Running Press, 1987), among other titles. She has also written for a variety of magazines, including *Victoria, Garden Design, Bride's,* and *Good Housekeeping.* She resides in New York City.

About the Photographer

Tony Cenicola is a photographer specializing in food, with forays into gardening, travel, and aerial work. His photographs have appeared in a variety of publications, including *Parenting, New York* magazine, *American Baby, The New York Times Magazine, Redbook, Town & Country,* and *New York Woman.* Among his book credits are *A Dash of Elegance* (Macmillan, 1994), *Heirloom Herbs: Using Old-Fashioned Herbs in Gardens, Recipes, and Decorations* (Villard, 1990), and *Berries: Cultivation, Decoration, and Recipes* (Bantam, 1989). He resides in New York City.